First World War
and Army of Occupation
War Diary
France, Belgium and Germany

61 DIVISION
Divisional Troops
Divisional Ammunition Column
25 May 1916 - 31 May 1919

WO95/3045/1

The Naval & Military Press Ltd
www.nmarchive.com
Published in association with The National Archives

Published by

The Naval & Military Press Ltd

Unit 10 Ridgewood Industrial Park,
Uckfield, East Sussex,
TN22 5QE England
Tel: +44 (0) 1825 749494

www.naval-military-press.com
www.nmarchive.com

This diary has been reprinted in facsimile from the original. Any imperfections are inevitably reproduced and the quality may fall short of modern type and cartographic standards.

Contents

Document type	Place/Title	Date From	Date To
Heading	WO95/3045/1		
War Diary	Bulford	25/05/1916	25/05/1916
War Diary	Bleville	27/05/1916	31/05/1916
Heading	War Diary Of 61st Divl Amm Column From 1st June To 30th June Volume 2		
Miscellaneous	Officer i/c RA Section 3rd Echelon		
Miscellaneous	Appendix I Ammunition Dump.		
Miscellaneous	A Form Messages And Signals		
Miscellaneous	61st Div Art Order No 5		
Miscellaneous	Appendix 4 S/66		
Miscellaneous	Appendix 5		
Miscellaneous	C Form (Duplicate) Messages And Signals		
Miscellaneous	Appendix 7 D A C		
Miscellaneous	Appendix 8 Transfer of 61 D.A.C. to new Billets.		
War Diary	Map France Sheet 36A. i30.c.8.3.	01/06/1916	11/06/1916
War Diary	R.9. b 9.6	12/06/1916	24/06/1916
War Diary	L26.A.8b	25/06/1916	30/06/1916
Miscellaneous	Nominal Roll Of Officers.		
Miscellaneous	War Diary For Month Of July 1916		
War Diary	Map Reference L 26 A 8.6 France Sheet 36 A 1:40,000	01/07/1916	31/08/1916
Miscellaneous	Appendix A Extract for orders for Tuesday 4 July 1916 by Lt. Col W.T. Cox R.F.A. Commanding 61st (S.M) Div-Ammn Column		
Miscellaneous	Appendix C Officers Commanding Sections	25/07/1916	25/07/1916
Heading	War Diary Of 61 DAC Aug 1st to Aug 31 1916 Volume 4		
War Diary	Map Reference L26.a.8.6 France Sheet 36a Coition 1:40.000	01/08/1916	28/08/1916
Heading	61st D.A.C Sept 1st-30th 1916 Vol. V		
War Diary	Map Reference L26.a.8.6 France Sheet 36a 6 1:40,000	01/09/1916	30/09/1916
Heading	61st D.A.C Vol.6 Oct 1st-31st 1916		
Heading	61st Div Art		
War Diary	Map Reference L 26. A 8.6 France Sheet 36a Coition 6 1:40,000	01/10/1916	28/10/1916
Heading	War Diary 1-30 Nov 1916 61st D.A.C. Vol VII		
War Diary	Map Reference L26 A 8.6 France Sheet 36 A Position 6 1:40000	01/11/1916	26/11/1916
War Diary	Map Reference V.6.c.9.1 France (Albert) Combined Sheet	27/11/1916	29/11/1916
Heading	War Diary 61 D.A.C. Dec 1st-31st Vol. VIII		
War Diary	Map Reference V.6.c.9.1 France (Albert) Combined Sheet	01/12/1916	31/12/1916
Heading	War Diary 61 DAC 1-31 Jan 1917 Vol IX		
War Diary	Map Reference V.6.c.9.1 France (Albert) Combined Sheet	01/01/1917	09/01/1917
War Diary	St Acheul Maizicourt	10/01/1917	21/01/1917
War Diary	Gueschart	21/01/1917	30/01/1917
Operation(al) Order(s)	61st D.A. Column March Order For 7.1.17.	06/01/1917	06/01/1917
Operation(al) Order(s)	61st Divisional Amm Column March Order For 081017	07/01/1917	07/01/1917

Operation(al) Order(s)	61st Divisional Amm Column March Orders For 8.12.14	07/01/1917	07/01/1917
Operation(al) Order(s)	March Order For 21st 1.17	20/01/1917	20/01/1917
Heading	61st D.A.C Period 1-28 Feb 1917 Volume X.		
War Diary	Gueschart [Reference Lens II France	01/02/1917	05/02/1917
War Diary	Longpre [Reference Abbeville Map	06/02/1917	16/02/1917
War Diary	Hangard	16/02/1917	19/02/1917
War Diary	Camp 84 Harbonnieres Reference Map Amiens 17 Scale 1/100.000	21/02/1917	27/02/1917
Miscellaneous	March Orders For 14th Feb	14/02/1917	14/02/1917
Miscellaneous	March Orders For 15th Feb	15/02/1917	15/02/1917
Miscellaneous	March Orders For 16th Feb 1917	16/02/1917	16/02/1917
War Diary	Camp 84 Harbonnieres Reference Map Amiens 17 Scale 1/100.000	01/03/1917	28/03/1917
War Diary	On Trek Pargny Falvy	29/03/1917	30/03/1917
Heading	61st Div Am. Col. Period 1st-30th Apr 1917 Vol. XI		
War Diary	Pargny Falvy	01/04/1917	01/04/1917
War Diary	Meraucourt Montecourt Monchy-Lagache	02/04/1917	30/04/1917
Heading	61st DAC Period 1st-31st May 1917 Volume 13		
War Diary	Reference Map France Sheet 62 C Sheet 66	01/05/1917	19/05/1917
War Diary	Amiens 17.	20/05/1917	21/05/1917
War Diary	Lens	22/05/1917	22/05/1917
War Diary	Reference Map Lens 11 Naours	23/05/1917	31/05/1917
Miscellaneous	March Orders For No. 1 Section	08/05/1917	08/05/1917
Miscellaneous	March Orders For 19.05.17	19/05/1917	19/05/1917
Miscellaneous	Marching Orders By Lieut. Col. F.G. Willock.	17/05/1917	17/05/1917
Miscellaneous	March Orders for 21st May 1917 By Lieut. Co. W.T. Cox. Comdg 61st Div Ammn Col	29/05/1917	29/05/1917
Miscellaneous	Marching Orders For 22nd. May 1917.	22/05/1917	22/05/1917
Miscellaneous	March Orders For 24th May 1917 By Lieut Col W.T. Cox Cdg 61st Divl Ammn Col	24/05/1917	24/05/1917
Heading	61st Div. Am. Col. Period 1st To 30th June 1917 Volume XIV		
War Diary	Reference Map Lens 11	01/06/1917	08/06/1917
War Diary	Reference Map France 51 B	09/06/1917	29/06/1917
Heading	61st D.A.C. Period 1st To 31st July 1917 Vol XV		
War Diary	Reference Map Lens II 1:100,000	01/07/1917	09/07/1917
War Diary	Lens II Hazebrouck 5a	10/07/1917	14/07/1917
War Diary	Belgium & France Sheet 27 N.E. Scale 1:20000	15/07/1917	31/07/1917
Miscellaneous	March Orders By Lt Col W.T. Cox D.S.O. Commdg 61st Div Ammn Col		
Miscellaneous	March Orders By Lt Col W.T. Cox D.S.O. Comdg 61st Div Ammn Column		
Miscellaneous	March Orders By Lt Col W.T. Cox D.S.O. Comdg 61st D.A. Col		
Miscellaneous	March Orders By Lt Col W.T. Cox D.S.O. Comdg 61st D.A.C.		
Miscellaneous	March Orders By Lt Col W.T. Cox D.S.O. Comdg 61st D.A. Column		
Miscellaneous	March Orders By Lt Col W.T. Cox D.S.O. Comdg 61st D.A. Col 15 July 1917		
Miscellaneous	Marching Orders for Tuesday July 31st 1917 By Lieut Colonel W.J. Cox D.S.O. Commanding 61st Divisional Ammn Col		
Heading	61st Div. Am. Col. Period 1-31 Aug 17 Vol 16		
War Diary	Reference Map Belgium Sheet 28 N.W.	01/08/1917	31/08/1917

Heading	61st DAC 1st To 30th Sept 1917 Vol XVII		
War Diary	Vlamertinghe Area	02/09/1917	17/09/1917
War Diary	Watou Arty Area	18/09/1917	23/09/1917
War Diary	St Catherine Arras	23/09/1917	24/09/1917
War Diary	Watou A.A.	22/09/1918	22/09/1918
War Diary	St. Catherine Arras	27/09/1918	30/09/1918
Miscellaneous	March Orders for H.Q. 61st D.A.G. By Captain T.R. Alston Comdg 61st Div Amm Col		
Miscellaneous	Appendix B Officers Commanding Sections		
Miscellaneous	March Orders for No 2 Section D.A.G. By Capt T.R. Alston Commanding 61st Divisional Ammn Column		
Heading	61st Divisional Ammunition Column. War Diary From 1st To 31st October 1917. Vol. 18		
War Diary	Ref Map 51b G.13.b	01/10/1917	01/10/1917
War Diary	L.6.2.2.5	01/10/1917	15/10/1917
War Diary	G.13.D.7.4 Sheet 51B	16/10/1917	30/10/1917
Miscellaneous	March Orders for Tuesday October 2nd 1917 By Capt T.R. Alston Commanding 61st Divisional Ammn Column		
Heading	Cover For Documents. Nature Of Enclosures. 61st DAC War Diary Volume 19. Period 1-30 Nov 1917		
War Diary	Anzin St. Aubin	07/11/1917	30/11/1917
Miscellaneous	March Orders By Capt. T.R. Alston Comdg 61st Div Amm. Col for 17th Novem 1917	17/11/1917	17/11/1917
Heading	61st Divl Ammn Column May 1916-May 1919		
Heading	War Diary 61st Div Am Col Period 1-31 December 1917 Volume 20		
War Diary	Anzin St Aubin	01/12/1917	19/12/1917
War Diary	Equancourt	20/12/1917	31/12/1917
War Diary	Cayeux	31/12/1917	31/12/1917
Miscellaneous	March Orders By Captain J. R. Alston for SAA Section 61st Divl Ammn Column	02/12/1917	02/12/1917
Miscellaneous	March Orders For 26th.12.17 By Col S.D. Browne C.B. Comdg 61st Div Ammn Col	26/12/1917	26/12/1917
Miscellaneous	March Orders For 301217 By Col S.D. Browne C.B. Cdg 61st Div Ammn Col	30/12/1917	30/12/1917
Miscellaneous	March Orders For 31st.12.17 By Col S.D. Browne C.B. Cdg 61st Div Ammn Col	31/12/1917	31/12/1917
War Diary	Cayeux-En-Santerre	01/01/1918	09/01/1918
War Diary	Roye	10/01/1918	11/01/1918
War Diary	Villers St Christophe	13/01/1918	31/01/1918
Heading	61st Div Ammunition Column 1st Feb 1918 To 28th Feb 1918. Vol. 22		
War Diary	Villers Ste Christophe	01/02/1918	27/02/1918
War Diary	Quivieres	01/03/1918	22/03/1918
War Diary	Etalon	23/03/1918	24/03/1918
War Diary	Fresnoy	25/03/1918	25/03/1918
War Diary	Andechy	25/03/1918	25/03/1918
War Diary	Bouchoir Laboissiere	26/03/1918	26/03/1918
War Diary	Courtemanche	27/03/1918	27/03/1918
War Diary	Morisel Castel	28/03/1918	31/03/1918
Heading	61st Divisional Artillery. 61st Divisional Ammunition Column R.F.A. April 1918.		
War Diary	Refce Sheet Amiens 17	01/04/1918	06/04/1918
War Diary	Refce Sheet Dieppe	07/04/1918	10/04/1918
War Diary	Reference Sheet Amiens 17.	11/04/1918	26/04/1918

War Diary	Hazebrouck	26/04/1918	29/04/1918
Heading	61st Div. Ammunition Column May 1918. Vol.25.		
War Diary	Hazebrouck	01/05/1918	05/05/1918
War Diary	Sheet 36a	06/05/1918	29/05/1918
Heading	61st Divisional Ammunition Column. Month Of June 1918. Vol. 26		
War Diary	Sheet 36a	01/06/1918	28/06/1918
Heading	61st Div. Ammn. Col. Vol 27 War Diary For July 1918. Vol: 27		
War Diary	Sheet 36a	01/07/1918	15/07/1918
War Diary	Sheet 36a Flechinelle	13/07/1918	22/07/1918
War Diary	Wardrecques Area Sheet 36a	23/07/1918	26/07/1918
War Diary	Sheet 27	27/07/1918	27/07/1918
War Diary	Sheet 36a	24/07/1918	25/07/1918
War Diary	Sheet 27	31/07/1918	31/07/1918
War Diary	Sheet 36a	31/07/1918	31/07/1918
Miscellaneous	March Orders By Colonel S.D Browne C.B. Commanding 61st Divisional Ammn Col		
Heading	61st D.A.C. Volume 28 1st-31st August		
War Diary	Flechinelle Estree Blanche Area	01/08/1918	01/08/1918
War Diary	Verchin	06/08/1918	07/08/1918
War Diary	Flechinelle Sheet 36a	07/08/1918	07/08/1918
War Diary	Boeseghem	10/08/1918	30/08/1918
Heading	61st Divisional Ammunition Column. War Diary For September 1918. Vol: 29.		
War Diary	Sheet 36a Boeseghem	01/09/1918	28/09/1918
Heading	61st Divisional Ammunition Column. War Diary October 1918. Vol. 30.		
War Diary	Sheet 36a	01/10/1918	07/10/1918
War Diary	Refce Sheet Lens 11	07/10/1918	10/10/1918
War Diary	Sheet 57 C	01/10/1918	10/10/1918
War Diary	Valenciennes	12/10/1918	13/10/1918
War Diary	Sheet 57b	15/10/1918	19/10/1918
War Diary	Sheet 57c	18/10/1918	18/10/1918
War Diary	Sheet 57b	19/10/1918	19/10/1918
War Diary	Sheet 51a	21/10/1918	27/10/1918
Heading	61st Divisional Ammunition Column. War Diary For November 1918. Vol: 31.		
War Diary	Sheet 51a	01/11/1918	18/11/1918
War Diary	400,000 Valenciennes	19/11/1918	28/11/1918
Heading	61st Divisional Ammunition Column. War Diary For December 1918. Vol: 32.		
War Diary	Sheet Lens 1/100,000	08/12/1918	28/12/1918
Heading	61st Div. Ammunition Column. War Diary For January 1919. Vol: 33		
War Diary	Sheet Lens 1/100,000	03/01/1919	31/05/1919

61 Div Am Col
Vol 1

61

Army Form C. 2118.

WAR DIARY
or
~~INTELLIGENCE~~ SUMMARY.
(*Erase heading not required.*)

Instructions regarding War Diaries and Intelligence Summaries are contained in F. S. Regs., Part II. and the Staff Manual respectively. Title pages will be prepared in manuscript.

May 16 to May 19

Place	Date	Hour	Summary of Events and Information	Remarks and references to Appendices
Bulford	25/5/16		The Column entrained at AMESBURY in 12 trains, the 1st train leaving at 3-40 am + the last at 3-55 p.m for SOUTHAMPTON, en route for FRANCE. The Unit was conveyed across the channel to LE HAVRE, in 3 boats, viz S.S. NIRVANA, S.S. ARCHIMEDES, and S.S. AUSTRALIND, comprising, 17 Officers other ranks horses, 179 vehicles, + the whole Unit assembled in No 2 Camp, BLEVILLE at 2-0 p.m 27/5/16	W.H.
Bleville	27/5/16		NIL.	W.H.
	28/5/16		NIL.	W.H.
	29/5/16		Entrainment orders received	W.H.
	30/5/16		The Unit proceeded from LE HAVRE in 7 trains the 1st train leaving at 7.54 am 30/5/16 + the last at 2-59 am 31/5/16 + detrained at BERGUETTE Map reference Squared Map FRANCE Sheet 36a O15 D54 + proceeded by march route to Concentration Area Map reference Squared map FRANCE Sheet 36a. I 29. D.55	W.H.
	31/5/16		NIL	W.H.

W T Coggs

Lieut.-Colonel, R.F.A.
Commanding 61st (S.M.) Div. Amn. Col.

T2134. Wt. W708—776. 500000. 4/15. Sir J. C. & S.

Vol 2

Confidential

WAR DIARY

OF

61st Divl Amm Column

FROM 1st June TO 30th June

(VOLUME 2)

Secret

(61st (S.M.) DIVISIONAL AMN. COL.
No. SWD/2)

Officer i/c
R A Section,
3rd Echelon

Herewith please War Diary from 1st to 30th June, inclusive

[signature]

Lieut. Colonel, R.F.A.
Commanding 61st (S.M.) Div. Amn. Col.

30.6.16.

Copy

Appendix I

R.A. Q/ 97/16
14. 6. 16.

Ammunition Dump.

305 Art. Bde.
306 " "
307 " "
308 " "
61 D.A.C.
Right Group (for attached batteries)
Left Group do.

(1) Further to my R.A. Q/ 97/15 of to day, Dumps of Artillery Ammunition will be established as follows — Authority XI Corps letter Q/145/79 dated 13th inst. — The following amounts include existing dumps.

	Rounds per Gun	
	H.E.	Shrapnel.
18 pr.	452	452
4.5" How.	500	

(2) The above dumps will be established in units of the 61st Div. Art. excluding the positions now occupied by attached Batteries, as follows:—

	18 pr.	4.5" How.
In gun positions	500 Rds. per gun	300 Rds. per gun
In "B" Echelon D.A.C. 1404	" "	200 " "

The ratios of natures of ammunition in the dumps will be as follows:—

18 pr.	50%	H.E.
	50%	Shrapnel
4.5" How.	100%	H.E.

(3) This dump ammunition will commence being drawn to morrow 15th inst. and units will draw from D.A.C. who will issue as available, until the dumps are completed.

(4) (a) These dumps will not be made at the gun positions of the attached batteries, viz:, C/158 C/174. D/159, A/167. B/163 D/179.

(b) These dumps will also not be established at the gun positions of the following units for the present:—
C/307 A/306 ½ B/306 (i.e. the half which is proceeding to a new position.)
C/306 will establish half the authorised dump at the gun position at present occupied by 1 Section.

(5) As the ammunition will commence being drawn to-morrow the 15th inst. it is a matter of extreme urgency that the structure for the dumps be completed at the earliest possible moment.
As a temporary expedient, duck boarding could be used as a base and tarpaulins as cover.
Tarpaulins as follows will be delivered by the 61 D.A.C. to the Wagon Lines of all units with the exception of those mentioned in paras. 4 (a) and (b) (except in the case of C/306 in which Wagon Line 1 tarpaulin will be delivered):—

2 tarpaulins — 16' x 16' per wagon line with above exceptions.

61 D.A.C. will use any tarpaulins required for the dumps in "B" Echelon.

Officers Commanding will advise this office if any additional tarpaulins are required.

Requirements such as timber, etc. will be submitted to the C.R.E. at LA GORGUE direct, and the necessary transport will be supplied by the 61 D.A.C.

(6) Batteries taking over gun positions in the 35th Div. Art. Area will take over the dumps in those areas, and care is to be taken that the amount of ammunition in these dumps is taken into account in establishing the new authorised dump in accordance with para. (2)

(7) The quantities of ammunition drawn to complete dumps in accordance with para. (2) will be drawn on Indents marked "For dump".

(8) Ordinary expenditure, and amounts required to complete Echelons to establishment will be drawn on Indents marked "EXPENDITURE"

(9) These two natures of Indents will continue to be used until the dumps are complete. Thereafter, ammunition to replace expenditure will be drawn in the usual manner, and Indents will not then need to be specially marked.

(10) Ammunition is to be constantly turned over by replacing expenditure, by drawings from the dumps at the gun positions and in the "B" Echelon, and replacing by ammunition drawn from echelons to replace expenditure.

Care is to be taken that a cyclic system is established to prevent dump ammunition remaining as such for too long periods.

(11) Ammunition dumps are not to be established inside towns or villages, but isolated buildings may be used if conveniently situated.

(12) The normal expenditure of 600 Rounds per Brigade per week for the present will not be exceeded.

(Signed) H.G. Rowe
Major
S.C.R.A.
61 Div.

R.A. H.Q.
61 Div.
14/6/1916.

Copy

"A" Form.

MESSAGES AND SIGNALS.

No. of Message

Prefix SM. Code IE p.m. Words 54 Charge

Office of Origin and Service Instructions.

X 61

Sent At m. To By

This message is on a/c of: Service.

(Signature of "Franking Officer.")

Appendix 2

Recd. at m. Date From By

TO 61 D.A.C.

Sender's Number. S.C. 1300 | Day of Month 15 | In reply to Number | AAA

Following copy of D.H.Q. telegram Q465 15th for action begins AAA Following wire from 11th Corps begins AAA Draw to-morrow at O.Z. for dump 6000 A 7000 Ax 1800 Bx aaa ends AAA Arrange accordingly addressed 61 R.A. repeated 61 Sub Park ends AAA

From 61 Div. Art.

Place

Time

The above may be forwarded as now corrected. (Z)

Censor. Signature of Addressor or person authorised to telegraph in his name.

* This line should be erased if not required.

(4198) Wt. W14042—M44. 300000 Pads. 12/15. Sir J. C. & S.

SECRET.

Copy 24

Appendix 3.

61st Div. Art. Order No. 5

June 16th 1916

1 The 61st Div. will take over part of the line held by the 35th Div. as far south as OXFORD STREET exclusive (S.5.c.4½.5½) on 16/17th

The additional front will form the Right Subsection of the Right Section which will in future be known as the NEUVE CHAPELLE SECTION. The other two Subsections will be the centre and left subsections.

2 The 183rd Bde. will take over the new front from 105th Bde. on the 16th. The 183rd Bde. will then have three Battalions in the front line.

3. Following units of 35th Divn. will be attached
To right Group – Z.35. T.M. Battery.
To left Group – Y.35 T.M. Battery

4 The relief of the 2. 18pr & 1 How. Batteries, 35th Div. and 1. 18 pr. and 1 How Batteries 39th Divn. at present attached to 61st Divn. will be carried out as shewn in attached tables.

5. The relief of the 3. 18 pt. Batteries in the 35th Divn. area by 2½. 18pt. Batteries of the 61st Divn. will be carried out on nights 17/18 and 18/19 as shewn on attached tables

6. After the regrouping of the Divnl. Artillery, which will be completed by night 18/19th the distribution will be as follows:–

Right Group Lt. Col. J. G. Willock } 305 Bde. 306 Bde.
Lt. Col. H Rochford Boyd } 1 Sect. (How) 307th Bde 2/35 T.M. Battery.

Left Group. Lt. Col. E.W. Furze } 307th Bde. (less 1 Sec. How.) 308th Bde. Y.35 T.M. Battery.

7. The G.O.C.R.A. 61st Divn. will take over the defence of the new portion of the line at 10.0 am. on 19th.

The Right Group Commander will take over the Defence of this line at the same time.

8. All ammunition in dumps and gun pits will be taken over by 61st Div Art at 12 noon on the 18th and receipts will be exchanged. Copies of receipts will be submitted to this office as soon as the ammunition is taken over.

9. Group Commanders will arrange to have a guard on any ammunition pits which will not be occupied after the redistribution until such time as the ammunition can be collected. Positions of such dumps will be reported to this office together with a statement of quantity and nature of ammunition in them.

10. The 61st D.A.C. will remain at PONT REQUEUL and will take over supply of ammunition in the new area at 10 am on 19th.

(Sd.) G. W. Meade
Major R.A.
Bde. Major 61st Div. Art.

Acknowledge

R.A. H.Q.
16.6.16.

Copy

Appendix. 4

No.6

Secret

S/66

1. Certain R. E. Stores will be loaded into G. S. wagons at LA GORGUE Station on the 17th and 18th inst. under the supervision of an R. E. Officer to be detailed by the O. C. "J" Co. R. E. and will be conveyed to dumps where they will be unloaded.

In addition to the stores, carrying poles and ropes will be distributed in the three sections on the 17th instant as under:

	Poles.	Ropes.
No. 1 Section	190	305
No. 2 Section	190	305
No. 3 Section	220	350

2. The C.R.A. will detail:

17th instant 66 G. S. wagons to be at LA GORGUE Station
18th instant 45 do. do. do. 7.30 pm.

The wagons will be grouped in three sections as under: Each Section will be in charge of an officer.

	No. 1 Section.	No. 2 Section.	No. 3 Section.
17th	21	21	24
✱ 18th	15	15	15

3. The G.O.C. 182nd. Brigade will detail fatigue parties as under to be at LA GORGUE Station at 7 30 p.m.

17th	3 officers	124 other ranks
18th	3 officers	84 other ranks

4. The G.O.C. 184th Brigade will detail a guard of 1 N.C.O and three men at each dump to take charge of the stores. The O.C. "J" Co. R. E. will detail 1 man to join each guard. Guards will mount at 10.30 pm each night and will be dismounted on the arrival of the carrying parties on the morning of the 18th and 19th instant.

5. After loading at LA GORGUE Station the convoy will proceed via. L.35. c. 6.3. to LAVENTIE starting at 9 pm in the order, No. 2 Section, No. 1 Section, No. 3 Section.

6 From LAVENTIE the convoy will move

No. 2 Section via. M.5.a.4.3. — M.5.c.7½.7½. — M.5.b.4.0. — M.6.d.1½.1. dump at entrance to PICCADILLY (M.6.d.5½.6.)

No. 1 Section following No. 2 Section to M.6.d.1½.1. — thence to dump at entrance to GREAT NORTH ROAD (M.12.b.1.7½.)

✱ Will be detailed by O.C. 61st Divisional Train.

Sheet 2.

No. 3 Section via FORT D'ESQUIN – M. 18. a. 1½. 9. – dump at entrance to MASSELOT STREET (M. 18. a. 1. 8.)

7. As wagons are unloaded they will return in groups of three independently to LAVENTIE, where the convoy will be reformed, moving by the following routes

No. 2 Section return by the route it came

No. 1 Section via. M. 12. b. 1. 7½. – M. 18. a. 1½. 9. – FORT D'ESQUIN – LAVENTIE.

No. 3 Section via. M. 18. a. 1. 8. – M. 17. d. 1. 8. – LA FLINQUE – LAVENTIE.

8. From LAVENTIE the convoy will return via LA GORGUE, route as in para. 5 to billets.

9. The O/C 61st Divisional Train will detail three Officers to act as guides, one to each Section.

10 No lights will be allowed until clear of LAVENTIE on the return journey.

11. Each loaded wagon will be accompanied by two fatigue men.

12 The O.C. "J" Company R.E. will arrange for the distribution of the personnel of his Company.

13 All ranks will wear gas helmets folded ready for immediate use.

(Sd.) C.C. Marindin
Lieut. Colonel
AA. & QMG, 61st Division.

17th June 1916.

Copies to G. No. 1
Q No. 2.
182nd Brigade No. 3
184th Brigade No. 4
Train No. 5
C.R.A. No. 6.
O.C. J Co. No. 7.

61 DAC.

For information and necessary action.
Please acknowledge.

(Sd.) T.R. Alston
Capt & ADC
61 Div. Art.

17/6/16.

Copy. Appendix 5

On the alarm of Gas being received at Column Headquarters your Cyclist Orderly will proceed from Headquarters to warn your Sentry who will immediately arouse all Officers and men of your Section. He will then proceed to the Sentries of the undermentioned wagon line and instruct them to arouse all officers & men of their unit and warn them of the Gas alarm.

No. 1 Section	A/305	R. 5. Central	No 2 Section	A/308	R.10. c. 4. 8
	B/305	R.16a. 8. 9.		B/308	R.4 d. 22.
	C/305	R.12. c. 8. 4.		C/307	R.10 8. 2. 7.
			No. 3 Section	B/306	R. 5. c. 2. 6
				C/306	R. 3. d. 3. 2

On receipt of these orders, cyclist orderly is to be instructed to return to D.A.C. Headqtrs to sleep, but before returning he will be instructed by you where these wagon lines are situated.

Please acknowledge.

(Signed) W.A. Lanham

Lieut. & Adjutant,
61st (S.M.) Divisional Amn. Col.

P.T.O.

Appendix 6

"C" Form (Duplicate). Army Form C. 2123 A.

MESSAGES AND SIGNALS. No. of Message.................

SM. 11·30 36 RA Gliddon

Charges to Pay £ s. d.

Office Stamp.

Service Instructions. F 61

Handed in at the..........Office, at..........m. Received here at..........m

TO 61st D.A.C.

Sender's Number	Day of Month.	In reply to Number.	AAA
SCT 325	twentyfour	—	
Number	2	section	of
the	DAC	will	move
from	its	present	position
R·10 B·25	to	its	new
position	L·36 A·8·2	between	2 PM
and	7 PM	today	

FROM 61 DIV. ART.

PLACE

TIME 11·20 AM.

GALE & POLDEN, LTD. PRINTERS, ALDERSHOT.
(69,017). Wt. 7981—448. 40,000 Pads. 4/18. W.

Appendix 7

Copy

D.A.C.

An offensive has commenced on the whole Western front. Every gunner and driver should be made to understand that by his individual work he is helping in the great battle.

5 German Divisions have been moved from the Western front to Russia to stem the Russian advance, which also commences to-day. This is the 1st time during the war that the Germans have had to conform to our initiative, and should mean the turning point in the war.

The 1916 class have already been absorbed in the German Front line, while the 1916 French Class are still in their depôt.

(Sd) G.W. Meade
Major RA
Bde Major
61st Div Art

24.6.16.

RAQ 227/4

Appendix 8

Copy No. 6.

Transfer of 61 D.A.C. to new Billets.

① H.Q., Nos. 1 and 3 Sections of 61 D.A.C. will transfer to new billets in accordance with following schedule, on the morning of the 26th inst., transfer to be complete by noon.

② No. 2 Section D.A.C. (which contains the Divisional Bomb-Store) moved to new billet at L.36.a.8.2. on 24th inst.

③ Schedule referred to in para. ①.

Unit.	Present position of Billet.	New position of Billet.	Remarks.
61 D.A.C. H.Q.	R.9.b.9.6.	L.26.a.8.6.	
No.1 Section.	R.11.a.1.1.	L.26.b.8.3.	
" 2 "	R.10.b.2.5	L.36.a.8.2.	Transfer completed on 24th inst.
" 3 "	R.3.a.9.2.	L.26.d.2.7.	

[signature]
Major.
S.C.R.A.
61 Div.

R.A.H.Q.
25/6/16

Copy No. 1 61 Div.
" 2. C.R.E.
" 3. 61 Div. Train.
" 4-8. 61 D.A.C.
" 9-12 305 Art. Bde
" 13-17. 306 " "
" 18-22 307 " "
" 23-27 308 " "
" 28. File.

61st Divisional Ammunition Column

Instructions regarding War Diaries and Intelligence Summaries are contained in F. S. Regs., Part II. and the Staff Manual respectively. Title pages will be prepared in manuscript.

WAR DIARY

or

~~INTELLIGENCE SUMMARY.~~

(Erase heading not required.)

Army Form C. 2118.

Place	Date	Hour	Summary of Events and Information	Remarks and references to Appendices
MAP FRANCE Sheet 36A				
I.30.C.8.3	1/6/16		Headquarters and details detrained at BERGUETTE and proceeded by road to HAVERSKERQUE and THIENNES. Headquarters established I.30.C.8.3 map FRANCE sheet 36A. following orders received XI Corps administrative standing orders. Routine orders, General Routine orders, Corps Routine orders, RA Routine orders Weather dry. Roads very rough but dry, Horse lines & Wagon Parks fair	WTC
I.30.C.8.3	2/6/16		Position unchanged, horse lines improved. Routine work. Roads fair weather dry	WTC
– do –	3/6/16		No change Weather wet horse lines & Roads bad.	WTC
– do –	4/6/16		No Change weather fine, horse lines & Roads bad	WTC
– do –	5/6/16		No change weather dull but dry Roads fair	WTC
– do –	6/6/16		No change weather wet Roads bad	WTC
– do –	7/6/16		No change weather dry Roads fair horse lines improving.	WTC
– do –	8/6/16		No change weather dry Roads fair	WTC
– do –	9/6/16		No change weather dry Roads better.	WTC

T2134. Wt. W708–776. 500000. 4/15. Sir J. C. & S.

61st Divisional Ammunition Column

Army Form C. 2118.

Instructions regarding War Diaries and Intelligence Summaries are contained in F. S. Regs., Part II. and the Staff Manual respectively. Title pages will be prepared in manuscript.

WAR DIARY

or

~~INTELLIGENCE SUMMARY.~~

(Erase heading not required.)

Place	Date	Hour	Summary of Events and Information	Remarks and references to Appendices
MAP FRANCE Sheet 36A				
I.30.C.8.3	10/6/16		Orders for 61st Division to relieve 38th Division received, giving map reference for new area of all Infantry and Artillery Brigades. Weather wet. Roads fair horse lines much improved	WT
I.30.C.8.3	11/6/16		Headquarters and No. 1 Section moved from THIENNES I.30.C.8.3 at 12 mid-night, to new area followed by No 2 at 12.15 am No 3. 12.30 am, No 4. 12.45 am	WT
R.9.b.9.6	12/6/16		All sections took up new positions, Hd Qrs at R.9.b.7.3 (map. 36a sheet). No 1 Section R.11.A.1.1. No 2 Section, R.10.b.2.6. No 3 Section. R.3.C.9.2. No 4 Section L.27.C.2.7 at 5.0 am communication established with 61st DIV.ART. Hd Qrs, weather dull, Roads ~~fair~~ v. bad, Fresh horse lines and wagon Parks left by outgoing unit in very bad condition, large accumulation of manure left.	WT
do	13/6/16		G.O.C. XI Corps inspected section areas. Orders received that ammunition dumps to be formed at Gun positions of Batteries, and that all ammunition for A. Echelon is dumped at No 3 section and transferred to wagons of Nos. 1 & 2. Sections No 1. Sections supplying Right Group. ie 305th & 306th Brigades & No 2 Section Supplying Left Group. ie:- 307th & 308th Brigades. Weather wet. Roads & horse lines bad.	WT

T2134. Wt. W708—776. 500000. 4/15. Sir J. C. & S.

3

61st (S.M.) Divisional Ammunition Column

Instructions regarding War Diaries and Intelligence Summaries are contained in F. S. Regs., Part II. and the Staff Manual respectively. Title pages will be prepared in manuscript.

WAR DIARY
or
~~INTELLIGENCE SUMMARY.~~
(Erase heading not required.)

Army Form C. 2118.

Place	Date	Hour	Summary of Events and Information	Remarks and references to Appendices
R.9.b.9.6	14/6/16	—	Orders from R.A. HdQrs that 1 Officer + 3 O.R to be attached for instructional purposes to 61st D.A.C from 35th D.A.C.	
			Orders received vide:- R.A.Q 97/16 dated 14/6/16 (copy attached, appendix 1) for formation of Ammunition Dumps and for building shelters for same	{R.A.Q. 97/16. appendix1 WRL
			Weather fine, but dull & cold, Roads fair	
R.9.b.9.6	15/6/16		12 Trench Mortars received & held by No 4 Section ("B" Echelon) pending instructions from RA HQ as to disposal. Ammunition received for Dumps as follows:- 6047 A. 4.789 AX. 700 BX. Pistol Webley 9 boxes. Mills Grenades 1512. Stokes 3" bombs 3.000. C.R.E. 61 DIV. indented on for sleepers & hurdles for dumps.	
			Orders received. Vide:- S.C.T. 300. 15th forwarding copy of D.H.Q telegram Q 465 (Copy attached, appendix 2) stating ammunition for Dump would be delivered as follows. 6000 A. 7000 AX. 1800 BX. Weather dry but dull. Roads fair	appendix 2) DHQ telegram Q465 WRL
R.9.b.9.6	16/6/16		Lieut - CURRAN + 2 N.C.O's reported for duty as instructors from 35th D.A.C.	
			Chaplain & Capt. B.C. Berry C.E. attached from R.A. HQ. G.O.C. R.A inspected section areas.	
			Orders received to send 8 Medium Trench Mortars to + Roads LAVENTIE	WRL

T2134. Wt. W708—776. 500000. 4/15. Sir J. C. & S.

4. 61st (S.M.) Divisional Ammunition Column

Instructions regarding War Diaries and Intelligence Summaries are contained in F. S. Regs., Part II. and the Staff Manual respectively. Title pages will be prepared in manuscript.

WAR DIARY
or
~~INTELLIGENCE SUMMARY.~~
(Erase heading not required.)

Army Form C. 2118.

Place	Date	Hour	Summary of Events and Information	Remarks and references to Appendices
Map. 36A FRANCE. R9 b 9 6	16/6/16		reference Map. FRANCE Sheet 36. SW. M4 D 77 to report to Lieut HOLMES. D.T.M.O. and to send all officers and men trained in French mortars to same Place. Orders received from RA HQ. regarding taking over line from 35th DIV. by 61st DIV and re-grouping of 61st DIV ART. (61. DIV. ART. order No 3. Copy 24. attached appendix No 3) 61. D.A.C. remain at PONT REQUEIL, Reference R9 B 9 6 and take over supply of ammunition in new area at 10.0 AM 19th inst. Weather fine Roads good.	61. DIV ART order No 3 appendix 3. W.L.
—do—	17/6/16		Order received from RA H.Q to detail 66 G.S. wagons to be at LA GORGUE Station at 8 P.M 17th inst for R.E fatigues and 45 on 18th inst for same purpose. Secret orders received reference this fatigue (Copy attached. appendix 4) Weather fine & sunny Roads good, Wagon Parks & horse lines better.	Secret orders re fatigues on nights 17-18 18-19 inst Appendix 4 W.L.
—do—	18/6/16		Drawing of dump ammunition from 61 Sub. Park Completed. D.A.D.M.S. and Divisional Sanitary Officer inspected Nos 1, 2 & 3 Sections, and reported as to the insanitary Condition of Billets and horse lines and advised move to more sanitary area if permission could be obtained from D.H.Q. Weather good. Roads good.	W.L.

T2134. Wt. W708—776. 500000. 4/15. Sir J. C. & S.

5/61 (S.M.) Divisional Ammunition Column

Instructions regarding War Diaries and Intelligence Summaries are contained in F. S. Regs., Part II. and the Staff Manual respectively. Title pages will be prepared in manuscript.

WAR DIARY
or
~~INTELLIGENCE SUMMARY.~~
(Erase heading not required.)

Army Form C. 2118.

Place	Date	Hour	Summary of Events and Information	Remarks and references to Appendices
Map. FRANCE Sheet 36A R.9.b.9.6	19/6/16		Orders received to send remainder of 4·2" French mortars to H.Q. Qrts. Left Group, complete with periscope boxes + tool boxes. reference M.4.B.4.3 Orders received that Lieut F.J. GATES reports for temporary duty to B/305 Battery Weather good. Roads good	WTL
— do —	20/6/16		Draft of 13 OR. arrived from BASE Havre and posted to Sections Frantic messages received from H.Q. Left Group to send up ammunition (12 midnight) & reporting that enemy had left his trenches, 2800 Rds dispatched to Wagon lines 307th & 308th Bdes, C Section used by 35th DIV Am Col as Dump taken over and removed to No. 4 Section Wagon lines, were re-erected as Dump shelter. Weather good.	WTL
— do —	21/6/16		Orders received that CO 61 D.A.C. responsible for warning all units in and around his area, if notice was given of Gas Alarm. Orders issued at once to all Sections (copy attached appendix 5) Weather good. Roads dry but very rough.	copy of Gas alarm orders appendix 5 WTL
— do —	22/6/16		Received 14 Ride and 2 LD horses from No 1 Coy A.S.C. Posted to Sections Normal Routine. Weather good. Roads under repair. Horse lines improving, but still bad.	WTL

T2134. Wt. W708—776. 500000. 4/15. Sir J. C. & S.

Instructions regarding War Diaries and Intelligence Summaries are contained in F. S. Regs., Part II. and the Staff Manual respectively. Title pages will be prepared in manuscript.

WAR DIARY
or
~~INTELLIGENCE SUMMARY.~~
(Erase heading not required.)

Army Form C. 2118.

Place	Date	Hour	Summary of Events and Information	Remarks and references to Appendices
Map. FRANCE Sheet 36A				
R.9.b.9.6.	23/6/16		Routine normal. Heavy Thunderstorms, & heavy rain, roads very bad again.	WL
— do —	24/6/16		Orders received No 2 Section to move from R.10 b 2 5 its present position to new position L 36. A. 8. 2 between 2 PM & 7 PM. reference SCT. 325 of 24th (Copy attached appendix 6) Weather showery. Roads bad, horse lines very bad. Report received reference an offensive on the whole Western front (copy of report attached, appendix 7) Verbal orders received from G.O.C. RA. that No 2. Section would take over Divisional Bomb Store, and form a large Dump for Bombs.	SCT d/d 24th appendix 6. Report as to offensive appendix 7 WTL
— do —	25/6/16		Orders received that Nos. 1 & 3 Sections & Hd Qrtrs move to new area (RAQ 227/4 Copy attached appendix 8) New areas. map FRANCE sheet 36A H.Q L 26 A.8.6	RAQ 227/4 appendix 8 WTL
L.26.A.8.6			No 1 Section L.26 B.8 3. No 2. Section. R.10 B.2.6. No. 3. Section L 26.D.2.7. Move completed from PONT RIQUEL to new areas by 12. noon 26th inst. Weather Showery, Roads good, new horse lines fair and an improvement on last areas, with exception of No 1. Section.	WL
— do —	26/6/16		Hd Qrtrs & Nos. 1 & 3 Sections moved to new areas, move completed by 12 noon. Weather wet. Roads in new area bad, & in bad repair.	WL

T2134. Wt. W708—776. 500000. 4/15. Sir J. C. & S.

Instructions regarding War Diaries and Intelligence Summaries are contained in F. S. Regs., Part II. and the Staff Manual respectively. Title pages will be prepared in manuscript.

WAR DIARY
or
~~INTELLIGENCE SUMMARY.~~
(Erase heading not required.)

Army Form C. 2118.

Place	Date	Hour	Summary of Events and Information	Remarks and references to Appendices
MAP. FRANCE SHEET. 36ᵃ L.26 A.8.6	27/6/16	–	Normal Routine. Weather bad. Roads bad. Horse lines very muddy. Draft of 10 O.R. joined from Base & Posted to No. 2. Section	WTC
— do —	28/6/16	–	No change.	WTC
— do —	29/6/16	–	No change. Lieut Col W. T. Cox was President of F. G. Court Martial at LAVENTIE.	WTC
— do —	30/6/16	–	2/Lieut H. G. Ansell, 2nd S. Mid Bgde & 2/Lieut A. J. Pyle 1st Wessex Bgde joined for duty. No. change. Weather good. Roads drying. Horse lines drying. Wind Strong S.W. to W.	

W. T. Cox
Lieut. Colonel, R.F.A.
Commanding 61st (S.M.) Div. Amn. Col.

T2134. Wt. W708—776. 500000. 4/15. Sir J. C. & S.

Instructions regarding War Diaries and Intelligence Summaries are contained in F. S. Regs., Part II. and the Staff Manual respectively. Title pages will be prepared in manuscript.

WAR DIARY
or
INTELLIGENCE SUMMARY.
(Erase heading not required.)

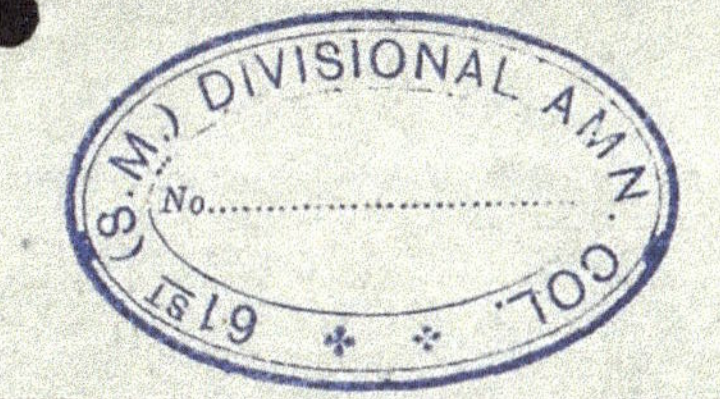

Army Form C. 2118.

Place	Date	Hour	Summary of Events and Information	Remarks and references to Appendices
			Nominal Roll of Officers.	
			Lieut. Colonel W. J. Cox R.F.A.	
			Lieut. W.H. Lanham Adjutant.	
			Captain T. S. Stafford R.A.M.C.	
			No. 1 Section Lieut. A. G. B. Spear — No. 3 Section Lieut. E. Yates	
			2/Lieut. D.G. Black — " A.S. Allen	
			" F. H. Gates — " F. G. Lesiter.	
			No. 2 Section Captain P. H. Ludlow — No. 4 Section Captain H.B. Dove	
			2/Lieut. G.H. Gibbs — Lieut. J.H. James	
			" ~~H.K.~~ Hawson — R. G. B. Chase	
			2/Lieut. H. L. Kenward.	
			2/Lt. H. G. Ansell.	
			" H. A. Pyle.	

T2134. Wt. W708—776. 500000. 4/15. Sir J. C. & S.

Officer i/c
R.A. Section

Herewith War Diary
for month of July 1916

J.R. Aston
Capt. & Adj.
for Lieut. Colonel, R.F.A.
Commanding 61st (S.M.) Div. Amn. Col.

1. 8. 16.

Instructions regarding War Diaries and Intelligence Summaries are contained in F. S. Regs., Part II. and the Staff Manual respectively. Title pages will be prepared in manuscript.

WAR DIARY
or
INTELLIGENCE SUMMARY.
(Erase heading not required.)

Army Form C. 2118.

61 Div Am Col

Vol III

Place	Date	Hour	Summary of Events and Information	Remarks and references to Appendices
Map Reference				
L 26 a 8.6	1:7:16	–	CAPT T. R. ALSTON reported for duty as Adjutant vice LIEUT W. H. LANHAM (Authy A/6/131 XI Corps 29:6:16)	
FRANCE	2:7:16	–	LIEUT W. H. LANHAM posted to No. 2. Section as officer in charge of Bomb stores with effect from 29:6:16	
Sheet 36a Edition 6 1:40000	"	10.30 pm	Severe Bomb detonation (map Reference about L.26.b.c.d.) no aircraft heard	
"	3:7:16	–	MAJOR-GENERAL H.F. MERCER R.A commanding artillery FIRST ARMY accompanied by BRIG-GENL R.C. COATES C.R.A 61. DIV ART and MAJOR H G ROWE STAFF CAPT R.A inspected D.A.C HEADQUARTERS and 4 Sections	APPENDIX A
"	1:7:16 – 5:7:16	–	NORMAL ROUTINE	
"	4:7:16		13 Reinforcements for D.A.C arrived LA GORGUE, allocated to Sections as follows (No. 1) 4 (No 3) 4 (No 4) 5	
"	6:7:16		Received from No. 1 Coy A.S.C 3 Ride horses, 2 L D horses, 6 mules (posted as follows H.Q 3 R. No. 2 Section 3 LD No 4 Section 5 LD	
"	7:7:16	9.15 am	No. 1 Section moved from L.26.b.8.3. to R.13.b 4.2.	
"	7:7:16		2nd Lieut C.A THURLEY reported for duty & was posted to No. 3 Section	
"	8:7:16		No. 1 Section took over 39 Division Ammunition Dump at R.32.b.9.9	
"	10:7:16		2 Lieut C.A THURLEY injured by fall from his horse & admitted to 2/1 F.A. & subsequently transferred to CASUALTY CLEARING STATION, MERVILLE	
"	5:7:16 – 11:7:16		Sections – NORMAL ROUTINE	
"	12:7:16		HEADQUARTERS D.A.C inspected by C.O prior to Route march	
"	11:7:16		LIEUT W.H. LANHAM & 12 men from No. 2 Section reported at HQ 182 Infy Bde for instruction in Bombs etc	
"	15:7:16		No. 1 Section moved from R 13 b 4 2 to L.32.b 5.9.	

T2134. Wt. W708—776. 500000. 4/15. Sir J. C. & S.

Instructions regarding War Diaries and Intelligence Summaries are contained in F. S. Regs., Part II. and the Staff Manual respectively. Title pages will be prepared in manuscript.

WAR DIARY
or
INTELLIGENCE SUMMARY.
(Erase heading not required.)

Army Form C. 2118.

Place	Date	Hour	Summary of Events and Information	Remarks and references to Appendices
Map Reference L.26.a.6.6 FRANCE 36c Edition 6 1:40,000	11.7.16			
	15.7.16		Sections - Normal Routine	
"	16.7.16		Major P.B. FOSTER temporarily attached to 61 D.A.C left for ENGLAND (under authority from G.H.Q)	
"	17.7.16		6 Ride Horses received from 9/306, & posted to No 4 Section	
"	"		C.O. received personal congratulations from G.O.C.R.A. on splendid work done by all Ranks during the last few days	Appendix B
"	18.7.16		3 L.D. Horses & 10 Mules received from Remount Depot GONNEHEM (H.Q. & remainder Nos 1.2 & 3. one L.D. Horse & 3 Mules each)	
"	"		13 men arrived from 48th Div Base Depot (3 men to Nos 1.3 & 4 Sections & 4 men to No 2 Section)	
"	21.7.16		2 Chargers, 2 Ride Horses & 5 L.D. Mules received from No 1 Coy A.S.C (1 charger & 1 Ride to No 3 Section, 1 charger to No 1 Section, 1 Ride & 5 Mules to No 4 Section)	
"	23.7.16	2.30 pm	Lt Gen R.C.B. Haking K.C.B. commanding XI Corps & accompanied by G.O.C. & G.O.C.R.A. 61 Div inspected Headquarters & Nos 3 & 4 Sections D.A.C	Appendix C
16/7/16 - 23/7/16			Sections - Normal Routine	
	22.7.16		15140 A, 5262 AX 378 DX received from 8 Division & dumped at No 4 Section	
	24.7.16		XI Corps Commander inspected No 2 Section & Divisional Bomb Store	
"	23/7/16 - 29/7/16		Sections - Normal Routine	
"	29/7/16		29 men posted to 3 Batteries 7/306 9/306 & 9/308, [illegible] orders from G.O.C.R.A.	
"	29/7/16		10 men & 1 NCO attached to Right group Headquarters for work in connection with O.P's	
"	29/7/16 - 31/7/16		Sections - Normal Routine	

Appendix A.

Extract from orders for Tuesday 4th July 1916 by Lt Col W. T. Cox R.F.A
Commanding 61st (S.M) Divl Ammn Column

205 Inspection. The Sections were inspected this afternoon by the Army Commander in company with the Brigadier General commanding Divisional Artillery & both officers expressed satisfaction at the condition of animals and camps and were appreciative of the work now being done. The Lieut Colonel commanding trusts that this standard of efficiency will not only be maintained but surpassed in the future.

[illegible]

Appendix B.

Extract from Orders for Tuesday 18th July 1916 by Lt Col. W. T. Cox R.F.A.
Commanding 61st (S.M) Divl. Ammn. Column.

285 Appreciation. The G.O.C.R.A. has instructed the Officer Commanding to convey on his behalf appreciation of the splendid work done by all ranks during the last few days and also desires that every Officer and man should be given as much opportunity as possible during the next few days for rest.

Appendix C

To:-

Officers Commanding,
Sections.

The Lieut. Colonel Commanding congratulates all ranks on the excellent report herewith attached and desires that it should be read to the troops on parade, also repeated in Unit orders. He feels confident that the standard of efficiency now existing will not only be maintained, but increased as time goes on.

It is possible that the Army Commander may inspect the Column at an early date. All ranks should be prepared for a surprise visit.

(Sd) J. R. Alston
Capt. & Adjutant,
61st (S.M.) Divisional Amn. Col.

D.A.C. H.Q.
26th. 7. 16.

61st Div. Art. RA.Q/436
25/7/1916

61st Division Q/587

Headquarters,
61st Div. Art.

The Corps Commander wishes you to inform Lieut. Colonel Cox, Commanding 61st Divisional Ammunition Column, that he was extremely pleased at his inspection of the D.A.C. on the 23rd inst., and that he considers it to be the best turned out Unit that he has seen, in the British Army in France.

(Signed) C. C. Marindin
Lieut-Colonel
A.A. & Q.M.G.,
61st Division.

Div. H.Q.
24th July 1916

(2)

Officer Commanding
61 D.A.C.

The G.O.C., R.A., 61 Div is very pleased to forward this recommendation, with which he agrees "in toto".

(Signed) H.G. Rowe
Major.
Staff Captain R.A.
61st Division.

R.A.H.Q.
25th July 1916.

Vol 4

CONFIDENTIAL

WAR DIARY

61 DAC

Aug. 1st to Aug. 31 1916

VOLUME. 4

Instructions regarding War Diaries and Intelligence Summaries are contained in F. S. Regs., Part II. and the Staff Manual respectively. Title pages will be prepared in manuscript.

WAR DIARY
or
INTELLIGENCE SUMMARY.
(Erase heading not required.)

Army Form C. 2118.

Place	Date	Hour	Summary of Events and Information	Remarks and references to Appendices
Map Reference L26.a.8.6 FRANCE Sheet 36a Edition 6 1:40,000	1.8.16-7.8.16		Sections - Normal Routine	
	7.8.16		2 R. 1 & 14 L.D. (Mules) received from No 1 Coy Div Train (allocated as follows: 2 R 1, 4 L.D No 1 Section; 6 L.D No 4 Section; 4 L.D No 3 Section)	
	2.8.16		3 officers & 41 other Ranks of X/61 Y/61 & Z/61 T.M. Batteries attached to 61 D. A. C (authority R.A. Routine orders No 164 of 2/8/16)	
	2.8.16		4 officers of D.A.C attached to Art Bdes, Lt R.G.B. CHASE attached 305 Bde, Lt A.S. ALLEN attached 306 Bde 2/Lt H.K. HAWSON 307 Bde, H.G. ANSELL 308 Bde.	
	5.8.16		CAPT BERRY (C.F.) temporarily attached 61 D A C admitted to 2/2 Field Ambulance.	
			Lt A.G.B. SPEAR, commanding No 1 Section app. temp. Capt from 23.7.16 (authority London Gazette)	
	7.8.16-13.8.16		Sections - Normal Routine	
	11.8.16		C.O received verbal instructions from Staff Capt R A to proceed with construction & undertake control of forward Bomb Store.	
	14.8.16	1.30pm	13 men reported for Medium Trench Mortar Course	
	15.8.16		2/Lt D.G. BLACK reported for a course in Heavy Trench Mortars	
	19.8.16		3 Section 31 Div D A C located at R.19.c.1.7. temporarily attached to 61 D.A.C	
	20.8.16		Brig Genl G.G.S. CAREY R A. held unofficial inspection of D.A.C, visiting Nos 3 & 4 Sections	
	13.8.16-20.8.16		Sections - Normal Routine	
	23.8.16		2 R & 17 L.D (Mules) received from No 1 Coy A.S.C (allocated as follows: No 1 2 R 3 L.D; No 2 6 L.D; No 3 3 L.D; No 4 5 L.D)	

T2134. Wt. W708-776. 500000. 4/15. Sir J. C. & S.

Instructions regarding War Diaries and Intelligence Summaries are contained in F. S. Regs., Part II. and the Staff Manual respectively. Title pages will be prepared in manuscript.

WAR DIARY
or
INTELLIGENCE SUMMARY.
(Erase heading not required.)

Army Form C. 2118.

Place	Date	Hour	Summary of Events and Information	Remarks and references to Appendices
Map Reference				
L26a 8.6 FRANCE	25.8.16		13 men returned from M.T.M Course, & reported to their Sections	
Sheet 36a	26.8.16		13 men as above reported to D.T.M.O, LAVENTIE	
Edition 6 1:40,000	25.8.16		2nd Lt D.G. BLACK reported from SCHOOL of MORTARS on completion of H.T.M. Course & is posted direct to D.T.M.O	
"	20.8.16 - 26.8.16		Sections - Normal Routine	
"	28.8.16		61 D.A.C (Nos 3 & 4 Sections) inspected by the XI Corps Commander Lt Gen Sir C.A. ANDERSON K.C.B. accompanied by G.O.C.RA & A.A.Q.M.G. 61 Div	
"	"	5pm	Draft of 7 new arrivals from No 1 Territorial Base Depot for posting to D.A.C	
"	"		Capt & Adjt T.R. Alston & No 1444 Sergt Jeffery W.G. reported for 4 days course of Physical Culture at L34c.5.7.	
"	27.8.16 - 31.8.16		Sections - Normal Routine	
"	28.8.16		4 officers detailed for attachment to Batteries returned to their own Sections for duty	

T2134. Wt. W708—776. 500000. 4/15. Sir J. C. & S.

Vol 5

CONFIDENTIAL

WAR. DIARY

61ST. D.A.C.

Sept. 1st - 30th. 1916

VOL. V

Instructions regarding War Diaries and Intelligence Summaries are contained in F. S. Regs., Part II. and the Staff Manual respectively. Title pages will be prepared in manuscript.

WAR DIARY
or
INTELLIGENCE SUMMARY.
(Erase heading not required.)

Army Form C. 2118.

Place	Date	Hour	Summary of Events and Information	Remarks and references to Appendices
Mazingarbe L26.a.8.6 FRANCE Sheet 36a Edition 6 1:40.000	1:9:16		Ammunition drawn for the first time from new Railhead O.Z.A	
	3:9:16		3 officers detailed for attachment to Batteries for month's instruction — 2/Lt A.S. PYLE B/306, Lt J.T. JAMES [illegible]/307, Lt F.G. LESITER [illegible]/308	
"	4:9:16		One officer (2/Lt G.H. GIBBS) & 3 Sergts detailed to attend 3rd Course in Physical Training for officers and N.C.O's at L.34.C.3.6 (period 4 days)	
"	"		Fatigue party of 25 men dispatched to ANNEZIN for work on FOSSE No 1, delivery of shale and slag to No 4 Section undertaken by 61 Sub Park	
"	6:9:16		4 Sergts & 16 gunners from D.A.C posted to 307 Bde, 2 Sergts 2 Corpls & 16 gunners posted to D.A.C	
"	1:9:16–6:9:16		Sections – Normal Routine	
"	4:9:16	7am	12 N.C.O's (4 each for No 1.3 & 4 Sections) detailed to attend Adjutant's 1st Course of Physical Training at L 20c 3.2	(period of [illegible])
"	11:9:16		14 N.C.O's (4 each for Nos 1.3 & 4 Sections & 2 for HQ) detailed for Adjutant's 2nd Course of Physical Training	
"	11:9:16		Fatigue party of one officer & 50 men detailed for 182nd Infy Bde fatigue in connection with transporting 2" T.M. bombs to front line. Party returned at 4 am 12:9:16	
"	7:9:16–12:9:16		Sections – Normal Routine	
"	11:9:16		25 men arrived from the 3rd Echelon & were allocated as follows (No 1) 6 (No 2) 7 (No 3) 6 (No 4) 6	
"	"		Trained Soldiers Table of Physical Training adopted throughout the D.A.C	
"	14:9:16		4 L.D. horses received from No 1 Coy A.S.C & allotted to No 4 Section	

T2134. Wt. W708–776. 500000. 4/15. Sir J. C. & S.

Instructions regarding War Diaries and Intelligence Summaries are contained in F. S. Regs., Part II. and the Staff Manual respectively. Title pages will be prepared in manuscript.

WAR DIARY
or
INTELLIGENCE SUMMARY.
(Erase heading not required.)

Army Form C. 2118.

Place	Date	Hour	Summary of Events and Information	Remarks and references to Appendices
Map Reference L26 a 8.6 FRANCE Sheet 36a Section 6 1:40,000	12:9:16			
	16:9:16		Sections – Normal Routine	
	17:9:16		4 Sergts & 16 Gunners returned to D.A.C from 307 Bde, 2 Sergts, 2 Corpls & 16 gunners returned to 307 Bde from D.A.C	
	18:9:16		19 men arrived from No 1 Territorial Base Depot & were allocated as follows (No 1) 5 (No 2) 5 (No 3) 4 (No 4) 5	
"	"		Captain G L S STOCKMAN took over command on posting of No 3 Section vice Lieut E. YATES	
"	19:9:16		No 1 Section moved from L.32.b 6.9 to R.11. Central.	
"	23:9:16		The following horses received from 308 Art Bde 5 Rides 11 L D allocated to the Sections	
"	"		3 O.R for Heavy T.M & 3 O.R for Medium T.M detailed to attend 3rd Course of Instruction assembly at First Army School, CLARQUES on 26th inst	
"	"		1 Q.M.S & 2 Drivers posted to No 2 Section from 305 & 306 Art Bdes	
"	16:9:16 – 24:9:16		Sections – Normal Routine	
"	25:9:16 – 27:9:16		Sections – Normal Routine	
"	24:9:16		1 L D horse received from 308 Art Bde & allocated to No 4 Section	
"	28:9:16		4 Sergts & 16 gunners to 308 Bde for instruction at the guns, 2 Sergts 2 Corpls & 16 Gunners from 308 Bde for attachment to D.A.C, both parties to be returned to their own units on 14th Oct	
"	28:9:16		Lt Col W.T. Cox proceeded to ENGLAND on 10 Days Leave, Capt T R ALSTON assumed command of D.A.C	
"	"		Party of Russian officers accompanied by A.A. & QMG XI Corps & A.A. & Q.M.G (61 Div) visited No 4 Section to enquire into the system of Ammunition Supply	
"	"		50 men detailed for 3 days fatigue with D.T.M.O.	

T2134. Wt. W708—776. 500000. 4/15. Sir J. C. & S.

Instructions regarding War Diaries and Intelligence Summaries are contained in F. S. Regs., Part II. and the Staff Manual respectively. Title pages will be prepared in manuscript.

WAR DIARY
or
INTELLIGENCE SUMMARY.
(Erase heading not required.)

Army Form C. 2118.

Place	Date	Hour	Summary of Events and Information	Remarks and references to Appendices
Map Reference L 26 a 8.6	28.9.16			
FRANCE	30.9.16		Sections - Normal Routine	[illegible]
Sheet 36a Edition 6	29.9.16		Party of Russian officers visited No. 2 Section & Bomb Store	[illegible]
1:40,000	30.9.16		Lt A.S. Allen posted from No. 1 to No. 3 Section S.A.C.	[illegible]
"	"		Lt F. G. LESITER & 2nd Lt A. J. PYLE returned from attachment to Batteries, & rejoined Sections	[illegible]

for J. R. Aston
Capt. & Adjt.

T2134. Wt. W708—776. 500000. 4/15. Sir J. C. & S.

Vol 6

CONFIDENTIAL

WAR DIARY

61st. D.A.C.

VOL. 6

Oct 1st - 31st

1916

61st Div Art.

Herewith War Diary for month of October 1916 please.

30. 10. 16.

T. R. Aston Capt Adjt
for Lieut. Colonel, R.F.A.
Commanding 61st (S.M.) Div. Amm. Col.

Instructions regarding War Diaries and Intelligence Summaries are contained in F. S. Regs., Part II. and the Staff Manual respectively. Title pages will be prepared in manuscript.

WAR DIARY
or
INTELLIGENCE SUMMARY.
(Erase heading not required.)

Army Form C. 2118.

Place	Date	Hour	Summary of Events and Information	Remarks and references to Appendices
Map Reference L 26. a 8.6 FRANCE Sheet 36a Edition 6 1:40.000	1.10.16		Sections - Normal Routine	
"	"		Inspection of Nos 1 & 2 Sections Horse lines & Winter Billets by Lt Col F.G. WILLOCK acting C.R.A, & Staff Capt RA	
"	2.10.16		" Nos 3 & 4 " "	
"	"		4 Reinforcements arrived from Base Depot & were posted to Headquarters	
"	5.10.16		2 Rides and 9 L.D. Horses received from No 1 Coy Divisional Train: 2 R 4 LD to No 2 Section, 2 LD to No 4 Section, 3 LD " No 3 "	
"	2.10.16	5.10.16	Sections - Normal Routine	
"	6.10.16		The CRE 61 Div Colonel J.E.G. DURNFORD with Staff Capt R.A inspected Dumps at No 4 Section & sites for proposed new Dumps at No 2 Section	
"	8.10.16		Lt Col W T Cox returned from leave & re-assumed Command of 61 D.A.C. vice Capt T R ALSTON	
"	6.10.16	9.10.16	Sections - Normal Routine	
"	9.10.16		Commanding officer, M.O. & 1 officer & 2 NCO's per Section attended Class of instruction in use of small box Respirator	at the Mairie LA GORGUE
"	9.10.16	12.10.16	Sections - Normal Routine	
"	10.10.16		Hardstandings of Nos 1, 2 & 3 Sections inspected by D AQMG 61 Div & Staff Capt RA	
"	12.10.16		Inspection of No 2 Section D.A.C by G.O.C.R.A	
"	14.10.16		" No 1 " "	
"	7.10.16		6 men returned from 1st Army School of Trench Mortars	
"	10.10.16		6 men transferred to D.T.M.O.	

T2134. Wt. W708—776. 500000. 4/15. Sir J. C. & S.

Instructions regarding War Diaries and Intelligence Summaries are contained in F. S. Regs., Part II. and the Staff Manual respectively. Title pages will be prepared in manuscript.

WAR DIARY
or
INTELLIGENCE SUMMARY.
(Erase heading not required.)

Army Form C. 2118.

Place	Date	Hour	Summary of Events and Information	Remarks and references to Appendices
Map Reference L.26.a.8.6 FRANCE Sheet 36a Edition 6 1:40.000	9.10.16		4 men for M.T.M & 4 men for H.T.M reported at 1st Army T.M. School CLARQUES.	
	13.10.16 - 15.10.16		Sections - Normal Routine	
	16.10.16		G.O.C.R.A accompanied by Staff Capt R.A inspected Nos 3 & 4 Sections & H.Q. D.A.C (Billets & Horselines)	
〃	16.10.16 - 18.10.16		Sections - Normal Routine	
〃	19.10.16		Lt Col H.T Cox removed to No 2 London Casualty Clearing Station MERVILLE	
〃	〃		Capt. T.R. ALSTON assumes command of 61 D.A.C during illness of Lt Col H.T. Cox	
〃	21.10.16		9 Mules received from No 1 Coy A.S.C & been allocated to No 3 & 4 Sections	
〃	20.10.16	1 pm	G.O.C.R.A inspected mules fitted with pack arrangements for carrying ammunition at No 2 Section	
〃	19.10.16 - 21.10.16		Sections - Normal Routine	
〃	12.10.16		Capt T.S. Stafford R.A.M.C. attached 61 D.A.C left on 7 days leave, Capt BANNERMAN R.A.M.C reported for duty in his absence	
〃	22.10.16		Capt T.S. Stafford R.A.M.C returned from leave, & Capt BANNERMAN returned to his own unit (2/1 F.A)	
〃	21.10.16		520 Howitzer Battery attached to 61 Div Art, and following personnel horses & Transport forming A & B Echelons transferred to 61 D.A.C No 1 Section 12 Drivers 24 L.D Horses 4 4.5 amm wagons. No 4 Section 12 Drivers 24 Mules 4 G.S. Wagons	
〃	24.10.16		4 Sections & H.Q. 61 D.A.C inspected by G.O.C.R.A in full marching order	
〃	22.10.16		Lt J.T JAMES transferred from No 4 Section to Headquarters as temporary orderly officer during illness of C.O.	
〃	25.10.16		Lt A.S. ALLEN temporarily attached from No 3 Section to No 4 Section	
〃	22.10.16 - 26.10.16		Sections - Normal Routine	

T2134. Wt. W708—776. 500000. 4/15. Sir J. C. & S.

Instructions regarding War Diaries and Intelligence Summaries are contained in F. S. Regs., Part II. and the Staff Manual respectively. Title pages will be prepared in manuscript.

WAR DIARY
or
INTELLIGENCE SUMMARY.
(Erase heading not required.)

Army Form C. 2118.

Place	Date	Hour	Summary of Events and Information	Remarks and references to Appendices
Map Reference L.26 a. 8.6 FRANCE Sheet 36 Edition 6 1:40.000	27.10.16–30.10.16		Sections - Normal Routine	
	29.10.16		Lt Col. W.T. COX VC assumed command of 61 D.A.C vice Capt T R ALSTON	
	27.10.16		CAPT P.H. LUDLOW proceeded on special leave to ENGLAND, LIEUT E. YATES posted to command of No 2 Section during the absence of CAPT P.H. LUDLOW on leave	
	28.10.16		2nd Lt C.R. LEEKE transferred from No 4 to No 2 Section to assist officer in charge of DIVISIONAL BOMB STORES	

T.R. Alston Capt RFA
for Lieut. Colonel, R.F.A.
Commanding 61st (S.M.) Div. Amn. Col.

T2134. Wt. W708–776. 500000. 4/15. Sir J. C. & S.

Vol 7

CONFIDENTIAL

WAR DIARY

1-30 Nov 1916

61st. D.A.C.

VOL VII

Instructions regarding War Diaries and Intelligence Summaries are contained in F. S. Regs., Part II. and the Staff Manual respectively. Title pages will be prepared in manuscript.

WAR DIARY
or
INTELLIGENCE SUMMARY.
(Erase heading not required.)

Army Form C. 2118.

Place	Date	Hour	Summary of Events and Information	Remarks and references to Appendices
Map Reference L 26 a 8.6 FRANCE	1.11.16 - 5.11.16		Sections - Normal Routine	
Sheet 36a Section 6	5.11.16		10 L.D Horses & one Ride received from 56 Division & allocated as follows { one Ride & 4 L.D No 3 Section; 6 L.D No 4 "	
1:40.000	4.11.16		B.G.R.A XI Corps & Staff Capt R.A 61 Div inspected No 1, No 2 Sections	
"	5.11.16 - 7.11.16		Sections - Normal Routine	
"	6.11.16		Six Day Slade fatigue at LABOURSE F.26.C.4.0, one officer & party of 40 men detailed for each day	
"	7.11.16 - 10.11.16		Sections - Normal Routine	
"	6.11.16		Course of Instruction for H.M.T.M's at CLARQUES Heavy 3 O.R Medium 4 O.R & one officer 2/Lt C.R LEEKE	
"	11.11.16 - 17.11.16		Sections - Normal Routine	
"	16.11.16		Horses of D.A.C inspected by D.D.V.S G.O.C.R.A inspected Horse lines & standings of all Sections	
"	17.11.16		61 Div Art order No 21 Copy No 20 subject Relief of 61 Div Art by 6 Div Art received	
"	19.11.16		61 D.A.C handed over supply of ammunition to 6 D.A.C at 12 noon, and moved out to	
"			rest at ROBECQ, Sections moved independently, 'A' Echelon filling up ammunition at	
"			HAVERSKERQUE en route.	
	20.11.16		61 D.A.C rested at ROBECQ	
	21.11.16		61 D.A.C resumed the march proceeding via BUSNES, LILLERS, BURBURE, ALLOUAGNE and	
	"		LOZINGHEM to AUCHEL	

T2134. Wt. W708—776. 500000. 4/15. Sir J. C. & S.

Instructions regarding War Diaries and Intelligence Summaries are contained in F. S. Regs., Part II. and the Staff Manual respectively. Title pages will be prepared in manuscript.

WAR DIARY
or
INTELLIGENCE SUMMARY.
(Erase heading not required.)

Army Form C. 2118.

Place	Date	Hour	Summary of Events and Information	Remarks and references to Appendices
	22.11.16	9.45 am	61 D.A.C resumed the march from AUCHEL, proceeding via CAUCHY-A-LA TOUR, FLORINGHEM, PERNES, VALHUON ANTIN to LA THIEULOYE	
	23.11.16	7.15 am	61 DAC resumed the march from LA THIEULOYE proceeding via MONCHY BRETON, ORLENCOURT, MARQUAY, La Belle Epine, LIGNY-St FLOCHEL, TERNAS, MONTS-EN TERNOIS, HOUVIN-HOUVIGNEUL to ETRÉE-WAMIN	
	24.11.16	8.56 am	61 DAC resumed the march from ETRÉE, WAMIN, proceeding via BEAUDRICOURT, LUCHEUX, HALLOY, CAUMESNIL to ORVILLE	
	25.11.16	8.39 am	61 DAC resumed the march from ORVILLE proceeding via TERRAMESNIL, BEAUQUESNE, RAINCHEVAL, TOUTENCOURT, CONTAY, VADENCOURT, HARLOY-BAILLON, SENLIS to HEDAUVILLE	
	26.11.16		61 DAC rested at HEDAUVILLE (Map Reference ALBERT combined sheet P.33.c. and d	
Map Reference V.6.c.9.1 FRANCE (ALBERT) combined sheet	27.11.16	8.30 am	61 D.A.C moved forward to V.6.c.9.1 (Map Reference of Headquarters) and took over following ammunition Dumps { 'A' Refilling Point X.9.c.3.4 CANADIAN DUMP W.24.c.5.2 / DONNETS POST W.12.d.9.3 D.A.C Dump W.27.b.8.8 }	
	"		Map References of Sections { No 1 Section P.36.d.1.1. No 3 Section V.6 central / No 2 " P.36.d.6.9 No 4 " P.36.d.6.1 }	
	28.11.16		Sections - Normal Routine	
	29.11.16 - 30.11.16		" "	

[signature] Capt. & Adjt.
for Lieut. Colonel, R.F.A.
Commanding 61st (S.M.) Div. Amn. Col.

Vol 8

Confidential

WAR DIARY

61. D.A.C.

Dec 1st – 31st

VOL. VIII

Instructions regarding War Diaries and Intelligence Summaries are contained in F. S. Regs., Part II. and the Staff Manual respectively. Title pages will be prepared in manuscript.

WAR DIARY or INTELLIGENCE SUMMARY.

(Erase heading not required.)

Army Form C. 2118.

Place	Date	Hour	Summary of Events and Information	Remarks and references to Appendices
Map Reference V.6.c.9.1 FRANCE (ALBERT) Combined Sheet	1:12:16 – 5:12:16		Sections – Normal Routine	
	5:12:16		CANADIAN DUMP (W.24.C.5.2) emptied of all ammunition & vacated by 61 D.A.C.	
"	"	1pm	2nd Lieut H.K. HAWSON & 2nd Lt H.G. ANSELL reported for duty to 306 Bde.	
"	"	"	1 officer (2nd Lt H.L. KENWARD) & 14 other Ranks proceeded to 5th Army School of Mortars VALHEUREUX on a Trench Mortar Course	
"	"	"	CAPT. H.B. DONE has been evacuated with Erysipelas (Map Ref P.36.d.6.1)	
"	"	6:12:16	2nd Lt G.H. GIBBS reported for duty to Lieut. E. YATES in place of 2nd Lt H.L. KENWARD at DONNETS Post W.12.d.9.3	
"	"	7:12:16	2nd Leave Party consisting of 5 other Ranks left for ENGLAND	
"	"	7:12:16	3rd Leave Party consisting of one officer (Capt T.R. ALSTON) and 10 other Ranks left for ENGLAND	
"	"	8:12:16	2nd Lt A.J. PYLE and Lieut R.G.B. CHASE reported for duty to 308 Bde	
"	"	9:12:16	Bombadier No 2 Section reported for Intelligence Course at St RIQUIER	
"	"	10:12:16	4th Leave Party consisting of one officer (Capt G.B. Spens) & 3 other Ranks left for ENGLAND	
"	"	12:12:16	1 Rid & 14 L.D. horses collected from VARENNES	
"	"	14:12:16	5th Leave Party consisting of one officer (Capt G.L.S. Stockman) & 10 other Ranks left for ENGLAND	
"	"	16:12:16	1st collection of bricks for hard standings from AUTHUILLE	
"	"	"	C.R.A. 61 Div & Staff Capt R.A. 2nd Division inspected Sections	
"	"	17:12:16	6th Leave Party consisting of one officer (Lt W.H. Lanham) & 3 other Ranks left for ENGLAND	
"	"	6:12:16 – 18:12:16	Sections – Normal Routine	

T2134. Wt. W708–776. 500000. 4/15. Sir J. C. & S.

Instructions regarding War Diaries and Intelligence Summaries are contained in F. S. Regs., Part II. and the Staff Manual respectively. Title pages will be prepared in manuscript.

WAR DIARY
or
INTELLIGENCE SUMMARY.
(Erase heading not required.)

Army Form C. 2118.

Place	Date	Hour	Summary of Events and Information	Remarks and references to Appendices
Map Reference V.6.c. 9.1. FRANCE (ALBERT) Combined Sheet	22.12.16		7th Leave Party consisting of one officer (Lt E. Yates) & 9 other Ranks left for ENGLAND	
"	19.12.16 - 23.12.16		Sections - Normal Routine	
"	23.12.16		Draft of 8 officers and 80 other Ranks for 50th Base Depot collected from Railhead	
"	24.12.16	10.30 am	G.O.C.R.A. inspected Draft at H.Q. D.A.C. previously to their being divided up between the 3 Art Bdes	
"	"		CAPT. W. H. WILLIAMSON reported for duty as o/c Horse Lines and was posted to No 1 Section for Rations & Quarters	
"	25.12.16		8th Leave Party consisting of one officer (Lt F. G. Rossiter) & 3 other Ranks left for ENGLAND	
"	23.12.16 - 29.12.16		Sections - Normal Routine	
"	29.12.16		31 L.D. Horses collected from No 1 Coy A.S.C.	
"	"		9th Leave Party consisting of one officer (Lt J. T. James) & 8 other Ranks left for ENGLAND	
"	30 - 31.12.16		Sections - Normal Routine	

[signature] Aston Capt & Adjt
Lieut. Colonel, R.F.A.
Commanding 61st (S.M.) Div. Amn. Col.

T2134. Wt. W708–776. 500000. 4/15. Sir J. C. & S.

War Diary.

61. Div

1 - 31. Jan 1917.

VOL IX

Vol 9

Instructions regarding War Diaries and Intelligence Summaries are contained in F. S. Regs., Part II. and the Staff Manual respectively. Title pages will be prepared in manuscript.

WAR DIARY
or
INTELLIGENCE SUMMARY.
(Erase heading not required.)

Army Form C. 2118.

Place	Date	Hour	Summary of Events and Information	Remarks and references to Appendices
Map Reference V.6.c.9.1 FRANCE (ALBERT) continued sheet	1.1.17		Sections – Normal Routine	
"	"		Preliminary orders received from R.A.H.Q with reference to move of 61 D.A.C on 7th inst	
"	2.1.17		9 other Ranks arrived from No 50 Base Depot, including QMS for No 1 Section	
"	5.1.17		11 other Ranks proceeded on Heavy & Medium Trench Mortar Course	
"	2.1.17–6.1.17		Sections – Normal Routine	
"	5.1.17		March orders issued for move of 61 D.A.C on 7th inst copy No 5 attached	Appendix A
"	5.1.17		10th Leave Party consisting of 9 other Ranks left for ENGLAND	
"	7.1.17		61 D.A.C moved to AMPLIER by 2 Routes { Route A HEDAUVILLE, FORCEVILLE, ACHEUX, LEALVILLERS, ARQUEVES, RAINCHEVAL, BEAUQUESNE, TERRAMESNIL & ORVILLE; Route B SENLIS, WARLOY, VADENCOURT, CONTAY, HÉRISSART, PUCHEVILLERS, BEAUQUESNE & TERRAMESNIL	
	"		The Echelons were completed to full ammunition * Establishment by the collection of A & BX ammunition at HÉRISSART	
	8.1.17		61 D.A.C moved from AMPLIER to OUTREBOIS via AUTHIEULE, DOULLENS, RISQUETOUT & OCCOCHES (Supplies drawn at CANDAS)	
	9.1.17		61 D.A.C moved from OUTREBOIS to MAIZICOURT via MÉZEROLLES, FROHEN le GRAND, WAVANS & BEAUVOIR RIVIERE	
	"		The B Echelon to St ACHEUL as above to FROHEN le GRAND, FROHEN le PETIT & BEALCOURT.	
St ACHEUL & MAIZICOURT	10.1.17		61 D.A.C rested at St ACHEUL (B Echelon) & MAIZICOURT (HQ & A Echelon) supplies for 2 days drawn at CONTEVILLE	
"	11.1.17		Supplies for 1 day drawn at CONTEVILLE	
"	"		Orders received from 2nd Corps to collect mails at St RIQUIER. Transport dispatched at once but on arrival mails had been forwarded to destination unknown	

* with the exception of SAA & Mills grenades which were handed over to 18 D.A.C

Instructions regarding War Diaries and Intelligence Summaries are contained in F. S. Regs., Part II. and the Staff Manual respectively. Title pages will be prepared in manuscript.

WAR DIARY
or
INTELLIGENCE SUMMARY.
(Erase heading not required.)

Army Form C. 2118.

Place	Date	Hour	Summary of Events and Information	Remarks and references to Appendices
St ACHEUL & MAIZICOURT	1:1:17		61 D.A.C rested at St ACHEUL (B Echelon) & MAIZICOURT (HQ & A Echelon) Supplies drawn at St RIQUIER	
"	8:1:17		11th Leave Party consisting of 4 other Ranks left for ENGLAND (Railhead ACHEUX)	
"	12:1:17		12th Leave Party consisting of 2 officers (Capt H.B. Dore & 2Lt G H Gibbs) & 7 other Ranks left for ENGLAND (Railhead AUXI-LE-CHATEAU)	
"	15:1:17		13 " " 1 officer (2Lt Locke) & 3 other Ranks left for ENGLAND (Railhead AUXI-le-CHATEAU)	
"	17:1:17		42 six mule teams lent to the 3 Infantry Brigades to assist them in moving into their Rest area	
"	"		14 six mule teams (No 2) with 2 G.S. Wagons carrying Forage & Rations proceeded under command of Lt J. T. James to	183rd Infy Bde MON PLAISIR
"	"		14 " " (No 3) " " Lt F. G. Lester to	184 Infy Bde GEZAINCOURT
"	"		14 " " (No 1) " " under command of CAPT WILLIAMSON to 182 Infy Bde FIENVILLERS	
"	16:1:17		mails collected at CONTEVILLE instead of St RIQUIER 17:1:17 mails again collected at St RIQUIER	
"	20:1:17		42 six mule teams returned from 3 Infy Bdes at CANCHY, DOMVAST, & MAISON PONTHIEU	
"	21:1:17		61 D.A.C moved from MAIZICOURT & St ACHEUL to GUESCHART via AUXI, LANNOY, WILLENCOURT, VITZ & VILLEROY	
GUESCHART	21:1:17	22:1:17	Rations & Forage delivered at GUESCHART by Supply Column	
"	19:1:17		2Lt PERROTT reported for duty & was posted to No 4 Section reposted later to No 2 Section	
"	23:1:17		Rations & Forage collected from Refilling point GAPENNES	
"	"		16 L.D. Horses & 8 mules received from A.S.C	
"	25:1:17		1 Corpl and 22 men arrived as reinforcements from the BASE	

T2134. Wt. W708–776. 500000. 4/15. Sir J. C. & S.

Instructions regarding War Diaries and Intelligence Summaries are contained in F. S. Regs., Part II. and the Staff Manual respectively. Title pages will be prepared in manuscript.

WAR DIARY
or
INTELLIGENCE SUMMARY.
(Erase heading not required.)

Army Form C. 2118.

Place	Date	Hour	Summary of Events and Information	Remarks and references to Appendices
GUESCHART	25:1:17		2/Lt F.J.E. Pratt & 2/Lt E.B. Waller reported for Duty & were posted to No 1 & No 4 Sections respectively	I
"	"		Lt W.H. Lanham was struck off strength on evacuation to ENGLAND	I
"	19:1:17		14 Leave Party consisting of 10 other Ranks left for ENGLAND (Railhead AUXI-le-CHATEAU)	I
"	22:1:17		15 " " 4 other Ranks left for ENGLAND (Railhead AUXI-le-CHATEAU)	I
"	26:1:17		16 " Lt Col W.T. Cox & 8 other Ranks " " (Railhead ABBEVILLE)	I
"	"		Capt T.S. Stafford RAMC M.O. i/c 61 D.A.C proceeded on Leave, Lt EVANS RAMC 2/1 F.A posted as locum tenens M.O	I
"	25:1:17	26:1:17	Re-organization of 61 D.A.C carried out, reducing number of Sections from 4 to 3	I
"	26:1:17	2.30pm	Surplus remaining after re-construction of personnel & horses, including Capt G.L. STOCKMAN and Lt E. YATES moved by march route to GRAND BELINVAL FARM near BRAILLY	I
"	28:1:17		Party of 18 other Ranks arrived as Re-inforcements from the Base, & were divided between the 3 Sections	I
"	"		2/Lt H. BUCKETT reported for duty from the 31st Divl Arty & was posted to No 4 Section	I
"	"		Inspection of animals of the D.A.C. by D.D.R. 5th Army, & A.D.V.S. 3rd Division as deputy for D.D.V.S. 5 Army	I
"	"		CAPT G.L. STOCKMAN admitted to Hospital (no change)	I
"	30:1:17		Convoy consisting of 52 horses, one G.S. wagon & 28 men including Lieut J.G. Lester & the Interpreter proceeded to BOUZINCOURT via CANDAS to collect 5 G.S. wagons belonging to the A.S.C	I
"			Lt C.E. BENNETT RE reported for duty & was attached for 3 days for the purpose of instructing signallers	I
"			A.D.V.S. 61 Div inspected horses of No 1 Section in connection with outbreak of mange	I

T2134. Wt. W708—776. 500000. 4/15. Sir J. C. & S.

[signature] Capt RA
i/c Cmdg 61 D.A.C

SECRET

61st D. A. Column.

March Orders for 7.1.17.

6.1.17

The 61st D. A. C will move from its present station on 7.1.16 to AMPLIER.

The move will be undertaken by two separate routes "A" via main ALBERT – DOULLENS road and "B" via WARLOY – HERISSART – BEAUQUESNE.

Capt. P. H. Ludlow will be in charge of the principle convoy and proceed by route "A".

Capt. G. J. S. Stockman will be in charge of the ammunition convoy proceeding by route "B".

ROUTE A All transport other than ammunition wagons and G.S. wagons required for A. and BX ammunit including H.Q.s and wagons supplied by Div. Train will proceed via HEDAUVILLE, FORCEVILLE, ACHEUX SARTON to AMPLIER. The head of the Column will be ready to move from the cross roads where WARLOY – MAILLY MAILLET road crosses the main ALBERT – DOULLENS road at 9.30. Sections will proceed to this point independently in the following order:– H.Q, Nos 1, 2, 3 and 4 Sections. All Sgt Majors with the exception of B.Sgt Maj. Hinton, will proceed with Capt Ludlow on route "A" and 2/Lt G. H. Gibbs will also accompany this party if available. On arrival of convoy at cross roads at MARIEUX a senior N.C.O from each Section will be sent forward to meet the advance billeting party at AMPLIER for the purpose of guiding their their Sections to billeting area.

The usual ten minutes halt per hour will be carried out throughout the march.

At the discretion of the O/C Convoy, an hours halt may be allowed for the purpose of watering and feeding horses. Strict road discipline will be maintained.

ROUTE "B" All ammunition wagons and G.S. wagons carrying A and BX will proceed independently from present Section positions to the Corps dump at HERISSART. The wagons should leave D.A.C. H.Q not later than 8.30 am as they are due to fill to complete Echelons Establishment at 12.30. The route taken will be via SENLIS, WARLOY, VADENCOURT, and CONTAY. Section Commanders and B.S.M Hinton, who will be in charge of No 2 Section wagons, will be responsible ~~for see~~ that strict road discipline is carried out and proper 10 minute halts taken after [illegible]

[illegible] their good [illegible] the [illegible].

[illegible] Doullens [illegible]

(Sd) [illegible] Knowles

Lt Col[illegible],
C[illegible] 61st R[illegible]

Copy No 1 to 1 Section
" " 2 " 2 "
" " 3 " 3 "
" " 4 " 4 "
" " 5 " R.S.M. [illegible]
" " 6 " Town Major
" " 7 " File

S/58

Gen. No. 5

6th Divisional Ammn. Column

[illegible] Orders

3 12 17

By [illegible]

The 6th D. A. C. will move from AMPLIER to OUTREBOIS. The Column will be ready to move at 11.15am and will proceed in order of Sections via AUTHIEULE, DOULLENS, HISQUETOUT, OCCOCHES to OUTREBOIS.

An advanced billeting party consisting of the Interpreter, R.Q.M.S. Spittle and 2 holders (as detailed today) will leave H.Q. for OCCOCHES at 9.30am sharp.

A convoy for the collection of rations and forage for 9th and 10th instant will report to Q.M.S. Mackenzie at the head of the Column on main AMPLIER – DOULLENS road at 7am. Sections will detail G.S. wagons as follows:-

H.Q.	1
No. 1 Sec.	3
No. 2	3
No. 3	3
No. 4	4

No. 1 Section will also detail a shoeing smith and No. 2 a fitter to accompany the party. Ration convoy will start punctually at 7am and proceed via AUTHIEULE, HULLEUX, BEAUVAL to CANDAS, where rations will be collected in accordance with verbal instructions given to QMS Mackenzie. The convoy will then proceed via FIENVILLERS direct to OUTREBOIS where each Section will arrange for a senior N.C.O. to report to QMS Mackenzie on No. 4 Section park at 12.30pm to take over rations and forage.

2/Lt C.H. [illegible] will be responsible for reporting at the railway station DOULLENS at midday and collecting the leave party consisting of 15 [illegible] and 3 other ranks and guiding them to the Column.

2/Lt A. M. [illegible] will report to the Town Major AMPLIER at 10am tomorrow morning after he has seen that all billets have been left in a satisfactory condition and will enquire as to whether any claims have been lodged against the Unit and whether a party need be left behind when the Unit moves.

Headquarters will arrange to collect mails while passing through DOULLENS and the least heavily loaded wagon must be used for this purpose.

Lt Colonel
Cdg 61st D A C

Copy No 1 to 1 Section
" " 2 " 2 "
" " 3 " 3 "
" " 4 " 4 "
" " 5 " R.S.M. Campbell
" " 6 " Town Major
" " 7 " File

S/58

61st Divisional Amm Column

COPY No. 7

March Orders for
8 . 1 . 17.

Ref Map LENS. 11 7 . 1 . 17

The 61st D. A. C. will move from AMPLIER to OUTREBOIS. The Column will be ready to move at 11.15am and will proceed in order of Sections via AUTHIEULE, DOULLENS, RISQUETOUT, OCCOCHES to OUTREBOIS.

An advanced billeting party consisting of the Interpreter, RQMS. Spittle and 2 horse holders (as detailed today) will leave H.Q for OCCOCHES at 8.30am sharp.

A convoy for the collection of rations and forage for 9th and 10th instant will report to QMS. Mackaness at the head of the Column on main AMPLIER – DOULLENS road at 7am. Sections will detail G.S. wagons as follows:-

H.Q.	1
No 1 Sec.	3
No 2 "	3
No 3 "	3
No 4 "	4

No 1 Section will also detail a shoeing smith and No 2 a fitter to accompany the party. Ration convoy will start punctually at 7am. and proceed via AUTHIEULE, HULEUX, BEAUVAL to CANDAS, where rations will be collected in accordance with verbal instructions given to QMS Mackaness. This convoy will then proceed via FIENVILLERS direct to OUTREBOIS where each Section will arrange for a senior N.C.O to report to QMS. Mackaness in No 4 Section park at 12.30pm. to take over rations and forage.

2/Lt C.R. Locke will be responsible for reporting at the railway station DOULLENS at midday and collecting the leave party consisting of Lt Lesiter and 3 other ranks and guiding them to the Column.

2/Lt G. H. Gibbs will report to the Town Major AMPLIER at 10 am tomorrow morning

This convoy will be met at CONTAY. by the Adjutant who will conduct the leading Section to the dump. As soon as each Section is filled it will proceed independently via PUCHEVILLERS, BEAUQUESNE direct to ORVILLE for AMPLIER. Guides will be found at ORVILLE to conduct Sections to their billeting area.

The opportunity will be taken to water and feed horses before proceeding on the trek after the Sections have filled up.

Two men per limbered wagon for the purpose of acting as loaders, will accompany each limber on "B" route.

Special attention should be paid to keeping well to the right side of the road. and also easing horses on hills by dismounting gunners.

Only 2 men per G.S. wagon will ride.

The first halt will be made at 10 minutes to the clock hour after leaving.

ACKNOWLEDGE.

Copy No 1 – No 1 Section
" " 2 " 2 "
" " 3 " 3 "
" " 4 " 4 "
" " 5 War Diary
" " 6. File.

[signature]

Lieut. Colonel, R.F.A.
Commanding 61st (S.M.) Div. Amn. Col.

Copy. 6

March Orders
for 21st 1·17

61st D. A. C. will move from its present area to new billets in GUESCHART tomorrow 21st instant by the following route - AUXI LE-CHATEAU, LANNOY, VILENCOURT, VITZ, VILLEROY to GUESCHART

~~No 1 Section~~ H.Q will move at 9am, No 1 Section at 9.30, No 2 Section at 10.0 and No 3 at 10.30

No 4 Section will go through MAIZICOURT and thence by the above route. The head of the column will be at HQ MAIZICOURT at 11 o/c.

All Sections will proceed under their individual Commanders

A senior N.C.O will be sent forward to GUESCHART to report to the Interpreter at the Church at 12 noon. Only one man will be sent

Copy	No 1	No 1 Section	Acknowledge
"	" 2	" 2	
"	" 3	" 3	
"	" 4	" 4	
"	" 5	War diary	
"	" 6	File	

H.R. Alston
Capt & Adjt
61st DAC

20·1·17

Vol 10

Confidential

War Diary

61st. D.A.C

Period 1 - 28 Feb. 1917.

VOLUME X.

Instructions regarding War Diaries and Intelligence Summaries are contained in F. S. Regs., Part II. and the Staff Manual respectively. Title pages will be prepared in manuscript.

WAR DIARY
or
INTELLIGENCE SUMMARY.
(Erase heading not required.)

Army Form C. 2118.

Place	Date	Hour	Summary of Events and Information	Remarks and references to Appendices
GUESCHART	1917			
[References LENS 11 FRANCE]	Feb 1st		61 D.A.C inspected by G.O.C.R.A 61 Div in full marching order	
〃	3		50 mules collected from ABBEVILLE and distributed between Nos 1 & 3 Sections	
〃 〃	2		27 Horses & 3 mules evacuated to M.V. Section at NEUVILLE near St RIQUIER by No 3 Section	
〃 〃	2		22 horses & 13 mules 〃 〃 〃 〃 〃 〃 〃 〃 No 1 Section	
〃 〃	3		Lt R G B CHASE A/306 reported for duty & was posted to No 4 Section	
〃 〃	4		2/Lt C.S CALLINGHAM reported for duty & was posted to No 4 Section	
〃 〃	5		61 DAC moved from GUESCHART to LONGPRÉ via MAISON PONTHIEU, YVRENCH, ONEUX, St RIQUIER YAUCOURT-BUSSUS, AILLY-le-Haut-CLOCHER, LONG and LONG-le-CATELET	
LONGPRE	6		G.O.C.R.A inspected Sections of D.A.C in billets	
[References ABBEVILLE Map]	〃		Lt E.S L.OSTLER reported for duty & was posted to No 1 Section	
	〃		2/Lt L.C LISTER 〃 〃 〃 〃 〃 No 2 Section	
〃 〃	5		Headquarters 308 Bde including CAPT THOMPSON RAMC & 2/Lt A.J PYLE, R.F.A, were attached to No 1 Section D.A.C for discipline Rations & Quarters	
〃 〃	7		CAPT LANDON D.A.Q.M.G (61 Div) inspected Horse lines & billets	
〃 〃	8		A.D.V.S. 61 Div inspected horses of No 1 Section segregated for suspected mange	
〃 〃	〃		Lt Col W.T COX returned from leave	
〃 〃	9		G.O.C.R.A & Staff Capt R.A inspected Harness & Horse lines	

T2134. Wt. W708—776. 500000. 4/15. Sir J. C. & S.

Instructions regarding War Diaries and Intelligence Summaries are contained in F. S. Regs., Part II. and the Staff Manual respectively. Title pages will be prepared in manuscript.

WAR DIARY
or
INTELLIGENCE SUMMARY.
(Erase heading not required.)

Army Form C. 2118.

Place	Date	Hour	Summary of Events and Information	Remarks and references to Appendices
LONGPRE	10:2:17		CAPT BLOXSOME A.V.C gave a lecture in the mayor's Parlour at the Mairie to the officers of the D A C	
" "			on "Horsemastership" followed by a practical demonstration in the Horse lines on the subject of Stable management	
" "	11:2:17		Inspection by the G O C 61 Div accompanied by G.S.O 1 and G.S.O 3 of Horses and lines of all Sections	
" "			Lieut. E. YATES & Lieut F. G LESITER reported for duty on completion of handing over details of	
			disbanded 3rd Section, Lieut F. G. LESITER was attached to No 1, & Lieut E. YATES to No 2 Section	
" "	13:2:17		5 officers & 51 other Ranks arrived from the Base & were attached to the D A C for the move	
" "	14:2:17	9 am	61 D A C moved from LONGPRÉ to ARGOEUVES via CONDE-FOLIE, HANGEST, BOURDON, YZEUX	
			BELLOY, LA CHAUSSÉE TIRANCOURT and St SAUVEUR arriving ARGOEUVES at 3 pm.	
	15:2:17	9.30 am	61 D.A.C moved from ARGOEUVES to AUBIGNY and FOUILLOY via LONGPRÉ-les-AMIENS, BERTRICOURT	
			CITADELLE D'AMIENS, CHAUSSEE St PIERRE, DAOURS, VECQUEMONT, arriving in the new area at 2.45 pm	
			March orders for 14' 15 & 16' not attached.	
	16:2:17	10 am	61 D.A.C moved from AUBIGNY & FOUILLOY to HANGARD via VILLERS BRETONNEUX arriving in new area at 1 pm	
* HANGARD	16:2:17 - 19:2:17		61 D.A.C rested in D staging area (HANGARD)	
" "	19:2:17		61 D A C moved to battle position, CAMP 84 on HARBONNIÈRES—ROSIÈRES ROAD. Route as follows.	
			AUBERCOURT, IGNAUCOURT, CAYEUX CAIX and outskirts of ROSIÈRES	
CAMP 84 HARBONNIÈRES	21:2:17		30 gunners & drivers from Draft received on 13:2:17 posted to 307 Art Bde	

* Reference map AMIENS 17 scale 1/100.000

T2134. Wt. W708—776. 500000. 4/15. Sir J. C. & S.

Instructions regarding War Diaries and Intelligence Summaries are contained in F. S. Regs., Part II. and the Staff Manual respectively. Title pages will be prepared in manuscript.

WAR DIARY
or
INTELLIGENCE SUMMARY.
(Erase heading not required.)

Army Form C. 2118.

Place	Date	Hour	Summary of Events and Information	Remarks and references to Appendices
CAMP 84 HARBONNIERES				
Reference – AMIENS Map 17 Scale 1/100.000.	22.2.17		Divisional Bomb Store moved from R.35.c. to W.17.a.5.0. Reference Map ROSIÈRES (combined sheet) 1st edition	[illegible]
	23.2.17 – 28.2.17		Sections – Normal Routine	[illegible]
	27.2.17		Inspection of Section horse lines by G.O.C.R.A	[illegible]

J. R. Aston Capt (Maj)
for Lt Col comdg 6. D.A.C.

S/66

Copy No 5

March Orders for 14th Feb.

Ref. Maps. AMIENS N+
N.W. Europe sht 3

The 61 D. A. C. will move from its present station to ARGOEUVES. Sections will move in order, HQs leading. The head of the Column will be at the cross roads at the junction of L'ETOILE-CONDE and HANGEST CONDE roads ready to move at 8.45 am. The tail of No 2 Section will be clear of the level crossing at that time. No 4 Section will remain in the side road indicated to O/C No 4 Sec. until No 2 Sec. has cleared this point.

The mange horses of No 1 Section will be led 50 yards in rear of the last wagon of No 4 Sec. and will be preceded by the A.V.C. Sergeant and followed by a N.C.O in order to ensure that no animals or men ~~being~~ are brought in contact with other Sections. These animals will follow No 4 Sec. to the place of assembly.

The route to be taken is as follows:- CONDE-FOLIE ~~FOLLE~~, HANGEST, BOURDON, YZEUX, BELLOY, LA CHAUSSÉE, ST SAUVEUR, ARGOEUVES.

A distance of 200 yards will be maintained between each Section.

The usual ten minute halts will be made. The place for the one hour halt will be notified from the head of the Column.

Refilling point for rations for 14th & 15th will be 1½ miles West of ST SAUVEUR - LA CHAUSSÉE road.

O/C Sections are, as usual, held responsible that their billets and horse lines are left clean and in good order.

Advance party consisting of the Interpreter, Lt F. G. Lester, RQMS. Spittle, and one mounted man from each Section, with necessary horse holders will leave HQs at 7.30 am.

No animals will be billeted during the trek. All will be placed on lines for the night.

ACKNOWLEDGE

Copy No 1 to No 1 Section
" " 2 " " 2 "
" " 3 " " 4 "
" " 4 " R.S.M. Campbell
" " 5 — War Diary
" " 6 — File

T. R. Alston
Capt & Adjt.
61 DAC.

Section commanders would do well to indentify place of assembly prior to the move, as the roads in this neighbourhood are liable to be confused.

T. R. Alston
Capt Adj

567

March Orders
for 15th Feb

Copy No 5.

Ref. Map AMIENS 14

The D.A.C. will move from its present stations to AUBIGNY tomorrow 15th instant. Sections will move in the same order as they did today. The head of the Column will be at the large crucifix adjoining No 2 Section wagon park. 205 yds due East of the entrance to the village, ready to move at 9.30

The route to be taken will be as follows: LONGPRE, BERTRICOURT, past the Citadelle in AMIENS & via BOULEVARD St PIERRE and main CORBIE road, VECQUEMONT.

Advance party composed as today will leave H.Q. Billet at 7.30 am.

ACKNOWNEDGE

[illegible]
Capt & Adjt
61 DAC

Copy No 1 to No 1 Sec
" " 2 " " 2 "
" " 3 " " 4 "
" " 4 " RSM Campbell
" " 5 " War Diary
" " 6 " File

S 68

March Orders
for 16th Feb 1917

Copy No 5

Ref. Map AMIANS.14

The 61 D.A.C. will move from AUBIGNY and FOUILLOY to 'D' Staging area tomorrow 16th instant. The place of departure will be at the Church FOUILLOY H.Q. will be drawn up on the RUE DE LA REPUBLIQUE, the head of No 1 Section will be at the Church and extending down the AUBIGNY – FOUILLOY road towards the hospital. Officers Comdg. Nos 2 and 4 Sections will follow No 1 Section and the whole will be ready to move at 10 am.

The advance party will ~~move~~ leave the Church at FOUILLOY at 9am. and will meet Lt R.S. Allen at VILLERS-BRATONNEUX at 10 am and will precede the Column to HANGARD.

ACKNOWLEDGE

J.R. Alston
Captn & Adjt
61 DAC.

Copy No 1 to No 1 Sec.
" " 2 " " 2 "
" " 3 " " 4 "
" " 4 " RSM. Campbell.
" " 5 " War Diary.
" " 6 " File.

WAR DIARY
or
INTELLIGENCE SUMMARY.
(Erase heading not required.)

Instructions regarding War Diaries and Intelligence Summaries are contained in F. S. Regs., Part II. and the Staff Manual respectively. Title pages will be prepared in manuscript.

Army Form C. 2118.

DA Column
Vol XI

Place	Date	Hour	Summary of Events and Information	Remarks and references to Appendices
CAMP 84 HARBONNIERES Reference map AMIENS 17 Scale 100.000	1:3:17 – 9:3:17		Sections – Normal Routine	
	9:3:17		Inspection of horse lines & stables by G.O.C.R.A	
	6:3:17		2/Lt G.S. PYLE posted from 308 Art Bde to D.A.C 8:3:17 2/Lt G.S. PYLE posted from D.A.C to 306 Art Bde	
"	2:3:17		2/Lt WALLER & 6 men returned from Course of TRENCH MORTARS (VALHEUREUX)	
"	8:3:17		2/Lt AUSTIN (No 2 Section) & 5 men proceeded on a Course of Signalling at SAINS-en-AMIENOIS	
"	2:3:17		1 Ride & 7 L.D. Horses received from 308 Art Bde	
"	9:3:17		2/Lt LYSTER (No 2 Section) attached to 307 Art Bde & reported for duty	
"	10:3:17 – 12:3:17		Sections – Normal Routine	
"	2:3:17		2/Lt E.S. OSTLER posted to 109 Siege Battery	
"	12:3:17		2/Lt MONTGOMERY reported for duty & was attached to No 4 Section D.A.C.	
"	12:3:17 – 21:3:17		Sections – Normal Routine	
"	16:3:17		2/Lt E.B. WALLER attached for duty to Trench Mortars	
"	19:3:17 – 21:3:17		All available G.S. Wagons detached for duty with Artillery Brigades & Engineers in connection with the advance	
"	22:3:17 – 27:3:17		Sections – Normal Routine	
"	28:3:17	2.30 pm	61 D.A.C moved from CAMP 84 HARBONNIERES via LIHONS & CHAULNES { Headquarters & B echelon to OMIECOURT, A echelon to PERTAIN	

T2134. Wt. W708–776. 500000. 4/15. Sir J. C. & S.

Instructions regarding War Diaries and Intelligence Summaries are contained in F. S. Regs., Part II. and the Staff Manual respectively. Title pages will be prepared in manuscript.

WAR DIARY
or
INTELLIGENCE SUMMARY.
(Erase heading not required.)

Army Form C. 2118.

Place	Date	Hour	Summary of Events and Information	Remarks and references to Appendices
On Trek	29.3.17	9 am	61 D.A.C moved from OMIÉCOURT & PERTAIN via MORCHAIN. HQ & B Echelon to PARGNY. A Echelon to FALVY	
PARGNY & FALVY	30.3.17		No 1 Section 35 D.A.C moved to VILLECOURT and came actively under orders of C.O. 61 D.A.C	
"	29.3.17		A.R.P established at MONCHY-LAGACHE under command of Lt. E. YATES with one officer & 28 O.R.	
"	31.3.17		A.R.P moved from MONCHY-LAGACHE to MERAUCOURT	
"	30.3.17		2 Lt. MONTGOMERY reported for duty at CORPS AMMUNITION DUMP, MESNIL-le-PETIT	

[signature]
Capt. & Adjutant,
61st (S.M.) Divisional Amn. Col.

T2134. Wt. W708—776. 500000. 4/15. Sir J. C. & S.

Instructions regarding War Diaries and Intelligence Summaries are contained in F. S. Regs., Part II. and the Staff Manual respectively. Title pages will be prepared in manuscript.

WAR DIARY
or
INTELLIGENCE SUMMARY.
(Erase heading not required.)

Army Form C. 2118.

Place	Date	Hour	Summary of Events and Information	Remarks and references to Appendices
On Trek	29.3.17	9am	61 DAC moved from OMIÉCOURT & PERTAIN via MORCHAIN. HQ & B Echelon to PARGNY, A Echelon to FALVY	
PARGNY FALVY	30.3.17		No. 1 Section 35 DAC moved to VILLECOURT and came actively under orders of C.O. 61 DAC	
"	29.3.17		A.R.P established at MONCHY-LAGACHE under command of Lt. E. YATES with one officer & 26 O.R	
"	31.3.17		A.R.P moved from MONCHY-LAGACHE to MERAUCOURT	
"	30.3.17		2 Lt. MONTGOMERY reported for duty at CORPS AMMUNITION DUMP, MESNIL-le-PETIT	

J. R. Aston Capt. & Adjutant, 61st (S.M.) Divisional Ammn. Col.

T2134. Wt. W708-776. 500000. 4/15. Sir J. C. & S.

95/12

CONFIDENTIAL

WAR DIARY

61st Div Am. Col.

Period 1st – 30th Apl 1917

VOL XI

Instructions regarding War Diaries and Intelligence Summaries are contained in F. S. Regs., Part II. and the Staff Manual respectively. Title pages will be prepared in manuscript.

WAR DIARY
or
INTELLIGENCE SUMMARY.
(Erase heading not required.)

Army Form C. 2118.

Place	Date	Hour	Summary of Events and Information	Remarks and references to Appendices
HQ & B Echelons } PARGNY A Echelon FALVY	1.4.17		Sections - Normal Routine	
MERAUCOURT MONTECOURT MONCHY-LAGACHE	2.4.17	11.30am 12 noon	[illegible] D.A.C moved to new area, A Echelon to MERAUCOURT via ENNEMAIN FOURQUES DEVISE & MONTECOURT [Cut to VILLECOURT] B Echelon & Headquarters & No 1 Section 35 D.A.C via FONTAINE-les-PARGNY, BETHENCOURT Y CROIX - MOLINEUX GUIZANCOURT, FLEZ MONCHY-LAGACHE; Headquarters remaining at MONCHY-LAGACHE B Echelon & No 1 Section 35 D.A.C proceeding to MONTECOURT	
"	3.4.17		Lieut E. YATES with A.R.P. personnel moved to new dump at CAULAINCOURT	
"	4.4.17		AMMUNITION DUMP at MERAUCOURT started, Lieut A.S. ALLEN officer in charge with permanent personnel of 22 O.R (Map Ref FRANCE 62c V 12 a 9 9½)	
"	5.4.17		One officer (2/Lt E B WALLER) & 32 O.R to NESLE as loading party at CORPS ammunition Dump	
"	6.4.17		6 O.R proceeded to NESLE on Signalling Course	
"	7.4.17		One officer (2/Lt AUSTIN) & 4 O.R returned from Signalling Course, MOREUIL	
"	[illegible].4.17		40 Re-inforcements arrived from the BASE & were divided up amongst Sections as follows No 1 Section 22, No 2 Section 3 No 4 Section 15	
"	10.4.17		Lieut E B WALLER & 10 O.R of the T.M personnel attached to D.A.C return to their [illegible] to Course at VAUX-EN-AMIENOIS	X/61
"	[illegible].4.17		Course in Morse Signalling assembled at Headquarters D.A.C for 12 O.R instructor [illegible] No 2 Section	
"	12.4.17		5 O.R. detailed for T.M. Course at VAUX-EN-AMIENOIS	

T2131. Wt. W708—776. 500000. 4/15. Sir J. C. & S.

Instructions regarding War Diaries and Intelligence Summaries are contained in F. S. Regs., Part II. and the Staff Manual respectively. Title pages will be prepared in manuscript.

WAR DIARY
or
INTELLIGENCE SUMMARY.
(Erase heading not required.)

Army Form C. 2118.

Place	Date	Hour	Summary of Events and Information	Remarks and references to Appendices
MERAUCOURT MONTECOURT MONCHY-LAGACHE	11.4.17		61 Divisional Bomb Store taken over by officer & personnel of 35 DAC	
	12.4.17	9.30 am	S A A Section & personnel of 61 D.B.S. proceeded to DOUILLY via FLEZ, GUIZANCOURT, QUIVIÈRES & UGNY the whole under the command of Lieut. E. YATES	
	12.4.17	midnight	61 DAC Ammunition Dump & supply of ammunition taken over by 35 DAC, the Ammunition Sections of the 61 DAC coming under the orders of the CO 35 DAC for ammunition supply but remaining under the orders of the 61 DAC for administration to take effect from midnight 12th inst	
	11.4.17		2 Lt PRATT (No 1 Section) & 10 O.R proceeded to NESLE, to replace 2 Lt WALLER & 10 OR proceeding on TM Course	
	12.4.17		Capt P.H. LUDLOW O/C No 2 Section proceeded to ENGLAND on leave, duties of O/C No 2 Section undertaken by 2 Lt G.H GIBBS	
	16.4.17		CAPT & ADJT T.R. ALSTON proceeded to ENGLAND on 10 days leave. Returned 28.4.17	
	11.4.17		One Corporal & 9 men arrived from the Base & were attached as follows 1 Corpl & 3 men to No 1, 2 men to No 2 & 4 men to B Echelon	
	23.4.17		CAPT A.G.B. SPEAR proceeded to ENGLAND on 10 days leave duties of O/C No 1 Section undertaken by Lt J.T. [illegible]	
	29.4.17		CAPT H.B. DONE proceeded to ENGLAND on 10 days leave duties of O/C No 4 Section undertaken by Lt A.S. ALLEN	
	30.4.17		RSM A.J.G. CAMPBELL posted to 35 Div ART on taking up commission as 2nd Lieut	
			Draft arrived from Base consisting of 1 Corpl 3 Bdrs 2 Signallers 20 Gunners 11 Drivers	

Army Form C. 2118.

WAR DIARY
or
INTELLIGENCE SUMMARY.
(Erase heading not required.)

Instructions regarding War Diaries and Intelligence Summaries are contained in F. S. Regs., Part II. and the Staff Manual respectively. Title pages will be prepared in manuscript.

Place	Date	Hour	Summary of Events and Information	Remarks and references to Appendices
MERAUCOURT MONTECOURT MONCHY-LAGACHE	28.4.17		2nd Lt MONTGOMERY returned from detached duty at A.S.P. MESNIL D.A.C.	
	30.4.17		Lieut J.C. FIELDING attached for duty to 306 Art. Bde & 2nd Lt BARNES to No 1 Section	
"	22.4.17		Divisional Bomb Store moved from DOUILLY to FORESTE (Lieut F.G. LESITER in command)	
" "	23.4.17		2nd Lt H.K. HAWSON transferred from No 2 to S.A.A. Section vice 2nd Lt C.R. LEEKE	
" "	"		2nd Lt C.R. LEEKE " " S.A.A. Section to D.B.S.	

for J.R. Aston Capt MSJ

Vol 13

Confidential

War Diary

61st DAC

Period. 1st - 31st. May 1917

VOLUME 13

Instructions regarding War Diaries and Intelligence Summaries are contained in F. S. Regs., Part II. and the Staff Manual respectively. Title pages will be prepared in manuscript.

WAR DIARY
or
INTELLIGENCE SUMMARY.
(Erase heading not required.)

Army Form C. 2118.

Place	Date	Hour	Summary of Events and Information	Remarks and references to Appendices
Reference map.				
FRANCE Sheet 62c Sheet 66E	1:5:17		Headquarters D.A.C V.18a 29. No 1 Section V.6.d 8.3. No 2 Section V.6.d 9½.2, B Echelon	V.11.b 3.5
"	"		S.A.A Section E.25a 3.8. D.B.S E16.c 9½.9.	
"	3:5:17		4 O.R. arrived with party of R.G. reinforcements for the 61 Div Art from the Base (1 Corpl S/S 2 Saddlers 1 acting Bombardier)	
"	"	11am	C.O. inspected S.A.A Section in full marching order at DOUILLY, afterwards proceeding to inspect Billets, cookhouses sanitary arrangements and horse lines	
"	"	4pm	C.O. made an informal inspection of D.B.S FORESTE	
"	"		2nd Lieut McCulloch & 33 O.R (T.M. personnel) attached for duty with D.A.C reported to D.T.M.O at ATTILY for duty	
"	4:5:17		2nd Lt P. PRATT & 30 O.R. returned from attachment at A.S.P. NESLE	
"	"		36 O.R forming original T.M. Personnel, or reinforcements for T.M's, reported for duty to D.T.M.O. ATTILY	
"	3:5:17		Lieut J.C. FIELDING (No 1 Section) reported to 306 Art Bde H.Q for duty	
"	4:5:17		Lieut A.J. PYLE (306 Bde) reported to D.A.C for duty & was posted to No 1 Section	
"	5:5:17		2nd Lt N.C. BARNES (306 Bde) reported to D.A.C for duty in place of Lieut J.C. FIELDING, & was posted to No 1 Section	
"	7:5:17		CAPT A.G.B. SPEAR returned from leave 6:5:17 Lieut E. YATES proceeded to ENGLAND on 10 days leave Lieut R.G.B. CHASE acting as O/C S.A.A Section during the absence of Lieut E. YATES	
"	8:5:17		2nd Lt N.C. BARNES transferred from No 1 Section to No 2 Section	
"	"	9.30	No 1 Section moved to VAUX via TERTRY and BEAUVOIS the original destination ETREILLERS was altered to VAUX on account of hostile shelling of the former place	

T2134. Wt. W708—776. 500000. 4/15. Sir J. C. & S.

Instructions regarding War Diaries and Intelligence Summaries are contained in F. S. Regs., Part II. and the Staff Manual respectively. Title pages will be prepared in manuscript.

WAR DIARY
or
INTELLIGENCE SUMMARY.
(Erase heading not required.)

Army Form C. 2118.

Place	Date	Hour	Summary of Events and Information	Remarks and references to Appendices
Reference map FRANCE Sheet 62C 66D	8:5:17		Orders for move of No 1 Section (appendix A) destination altered from ETREILLERS to VAUX by verbal order from 35 D.A.C	J
"	"		No 1 Section is transferred for ammunition supply from 35 D.A.C to 32 D.A.C but remains under orders of 61 D.A.C for administration	J
"	7:5:17		Inspection of all gas helmets in the unit by a Corporal from the gas School	J
"	13:5:17		2/Lt ANSELL and 47 O.R for 61 DIV ART arrived from the Base	J
"	"		2/Lt ANSELL posted to B Echelon	J
"	16:5:17		30 mules for 61 D.A.C collected from LA CHAPELLETTE & divided equally between Nos 1 & 2 Sections	J
"	"		82 Horses collected by party found by D.A.C from LA CHAPELLETTE and handed over to 306 Art Bde at TERTRY	J
"	17:5:17		185 animals were loaned from the B Echelon to various units of the Division under orders received from 61 Div (Q)	J
"	"		The following personnel & horses arrived from 19 Reserve PARK to make the B Echelon 1 officer 63 Other Ranks Horses 98 H.D 4 Rides	
"	19:5:17	5.45 am	61 D.A.C moved to ROUY-LE-GRAND, Route taken by H.Q. No 2 Section & B Echelon FLEZ, GUIZANCOURT, CROIX MOLIGNAUX, Y, VILLECOURT BETHENCOURT, No 1 Section from VAUX to ROUY-LE-GRAND via GERMAINE, FORESTE DOUILLY where the S.A.A Section joined the column, MATIGNY, Y, as above.	J Appendix B
AMIENS 17	20:5:17	5.30 am	61 D.A.C moved from ROUY-le-GRAND to CAYEUX-EN-SANTERRE via MESNIL-ST-NICAISE, MESNIL-LE-PETIT, MANICOURT, CURCHY, PUZEAUX, PUNCHY, HALLU, CHILLY, MAUCOURT, MÉHARICOURT ROSIÈRES and CAIX	Appendix C
"	21:5:17	5.50 am	61 D.A.C moved from CAYEUX, H.Q. & A Echelon to GLISY, S.A.A Section & B Echelon to BLANGY-TRONVILLE via HIENCOURT, MARCELCAVE VILLERS BRETONNEUX & PETIT BLANGY	Appx. D
LENS 11	22.5.17	6 am	61 D.A.C moved to NAOURS via LONGUEAU, AMIENS, LONGCHAMPS & FLESSELLES	Appendix E

T2134. Wt. W708–776. 500000. 4/15. Sir J. C. & S.

Army Form C. 2118.

Instructions regarding War Diaries and Intelligence Summaries are contained in F. S. Regs., Part II. and the Staff Manual respectively. Title pages will be prepared in manuscript.

WAR DIARY
or
INTELLIGENCE SUMMARY.
(Erase heading not required.)

Place	Date	Hour	Summary of Events and Information	Remarks and references to Appendices
Reference map LENS 11				
NAOURS	23.5.17		61 D.A.C rested at NAOURS	Appendix F.
	24.5.17	6 am	61 D.A.C moved from NAOURS {HQ A Echelon to HEM {S.A.A Section B Echelon to HARDINVAL. Route taken TALMAS, LA VICOGNE, VERT GALANT, BEAUVAL, BAGNEUX, GÉZAINCOURT & BRETEL	
	25.5.17		Owing to an outbreak of mumps orders were received from 61 DIV ART for the move of the B Echelon & S.A.A Section to BOISBERGUES	
	"	10 am	B Echelon & S.A.A Section moved from HARDINVAL to BOISBERGUES via HEM, RECMENIL, OCCOCHES, OUTREBOIS & LE QUESNEL FARM	
	28.5.17		G.O.C.R.A 61 Div accompanied by Staff Capt R.A inspected Sections of D.A.C at BOISBERGUES & HEM	
	29.5.17		Lieuts LESITER & LEEKE & 12 O.R. forming personnel of DIV BOMB STORE, proceeded to WARLUS by motor lorry (authority - 61 Div Q 341 - 28.5.17)	
	30.5.17		G.O.C.R.A inspected all the animals in Section Parks in the morning and Sections in Drill order in the afternoon	
	31.5.17		3 NCOs & 32 men from TRENCH MORTARS attached for duty to S.A.A SECTION at BOISBERGUES	

[illegible signature]
Capt & Adjt.
for Lieut. Colonel, R.F.A.
Commanding 61st (S.M.) Div. Amn. Col.

T2134. Wt. W708-776. 500000. 4/15. Sir J. C. & S.

Appendix A

March Orders for No 1 Section.

8th 5. 1917

No 1 Section will move tomorrow the 8th from present station to ETREILLERS in accordance with orders received from R.A. 35th Division, when this Section will come under the orders of the 32nd Divn Amm. Col. for ammunition supply to the 306th Art. Bde: the Section remaining under the orders of 61st D.A.C. for purposes of administration as heretofore.

The Section will proceed from MERAUCOURT via TERTRY and BEAUVOIS. The Column will be drawn up on the MERAUCOURT-TERTRY road ready to move at 9.30 am with the tail of the Column clear of the old ammunition dump opposite No 2 Section.

On arrival at ETREILLERS, the O/C will report to an officer of the 32nd D.A.C.

The Section will move with empty wagons.

2 G S wagon from H.Q, 2 from S.A.A Section and 2 from 'B' Echelon will report to O/C No 1 Section at 6.30 am to assist in moving the Section. These wagons will return to their respective Sections on arrival at ETREILLERS.

The Colonel will inspect the Section at 9.30 am on the MERAUCOURT-TERTRY road prior to departure.

A guide will report at the supply dump W. 9. c. 3. 8 tomorrow morning to conduct supplies to ETREILLES.

ACKNOWLEDGE

J.R. Aston
Capt & Adjt
61 DAC

DAC HQ
7 5 17

Appendix 'B'

March Orders for 19.5.17

Ref. map FRANCE sheet 62c [illegible]

The 61st D. A. C. will move from its present station to ROUY LE GRAND. The Column will move in 2 parties as follows:–

'A' Party Under command of Capt. Fiddes	'B' Party Under command of Capt. Spear
H.Q.	No. 1 Section
No. 2 Section	S.A.A. Section
'B' Echelon.	D. G. S.

'A' party will be ready to move at 5.30am H.Q. being at FLEZ, No. 2 Section and 'B' Echelon following immediately in rear at intervals of 200 yards between Sections. The Column should be in motion by 5.45am.

The route to be taken is as follows:– FLEZ GUIZANCOURT, CROIX MOLIGNAUX, Y, VILLECOURT, BETHENCOURT, ROUY LE GRAND.

No. 1 Section will leave VAUX at 6am and proceed under the orders of Capt. A.G.B. Spear to ROUY LE GRAND via GERMAINE, FORESTE by road N of River Germaine to DOUILLY.

S.A.A. Section will remain in their wagon park ready to move at 7am.

O/C S.A.A. Section will send a mounted orderly to O/C No. 1 Section at point R.16 A.6.5

The S.A.A. Section will follow immediately in rear of No. 1 Section leaving an interval of 200 yds.

'B' party will then proceed to ROUY LE GRAND via MATIGNY, Y, VILLECOURT and BETHENCOURT.

The usual halts of 10 minutes will be made at 10 minutes to the hour.

An advance party consisting of the Interpreter & Sgt Montgomery with horse holders and a mounted man from No 2 Sec. and 'B' Echelon will leave HQ mess at MONCHY LAGACHE at 2.30 pm on the afternoon of the 18th. A mounted man from No 1 Section and S.A.A. Section will report to the Interpreter at the Church ROUY LE GRAND at 4.30 on the same afternoon. Every man of the advance party should be in possession of the actual numbers of his own Section both in regard to personnel and animals; the figures to be available for the Interpreter if required. The figures for the B Echelon will also include the 19th Reserve Park. The advance party will be on the BETHENCOURT side of the Somme Canal to act as guides to Sections on the morning of the 19th. The advance party [illegible] rations forage and blankets.

ACKNOWLEDGE

[illegible signature]

MARCHING ORDERS

by

Lieut. Col. F.G. WILLOCK. Comdg. 306th Bde. R. F. A.

Reference Maps : ST QUENTIN 18. 1/100,000
AMIENS 17. 1/100,000

1. The Brigade will leave this area on the 19th MAY 1917.

2. H.Q. Staff will parade at WATERING PLACE, EAST of X ROADS ETTREILLERS, and move off at 4.15 a.m.

3. The Head of the Column (H.Q. Staff) will be at JUNCTION of MAIN ROAD from FORESTE at the point where it joins the ST. QUENTIN - HAM ROAD at 5.35 a.m.

4. Batteries will follow in the order undermentioned :

   A/306
   B/306
   C/306
   D/306

   with a distance of 200^{x} between each battery.

5. Column will move off at 5.45 a.m. Watches will be synchronised at 7 p.m. on the 18th instant.

6. Route : Via VILLERS ST. CHRISTOPHE
   SANCOURT
   MAZAGNY
   TOULLE
   MATIGNY
   Y
   BETHENCOURT
   ROUY LE GRAND (billetting area)

7. Reconnoitreing officer will report to O.C. Brigade at head of column at 5.35 a.m.

8. Each battery will detail billetting officer, who will report to Brigade Orderly Officer (2/Lt. F.J. BALY) at head of column at 5.35 a.m.

9. Each Unit will detail a Rear Party under an officer, who will be responsible that all camps are left thoroughly clean. They will report to the adjutant such is the case on joining the Column.

10. Baggage wagons will be brigaded in rear of the column. Cyclists will be in rear of baggage wagons.

11. A/306 will detail an Officer to be i/c of Baggage wagons and cyclists. B/306 will detail Reconnoitreing officer.

12. One officer from 61st D.A.C.
    One officer from No. 1 Co. Div. Train } will meet 2/Lt. F.J. BALY at 8 a.m. on the 19th instant at the CHURCH, ROUY LE GRAND.

13. Refilling Point, 19th May 1917 : On HAM - NESTLE ROAD, just outside NESTLE on arrival at ROUY LE GRAND.

F.J. Baly 2/Lt
for Lieut. Colonel.
Comdg. 306th Bde. R.F.A.

17th May 1917.

Copy No. 7

Appendix C

M A R C H   O R D E R S
by
Lieut.Co. W.T.Cox.
Comdg. 61st Div. Amm. Col.
for
20th May 1917

Reference Map France 62d Ed.1
Amiens 17.

The 61st D.A.C. will move from this area to CAYEUX.

The Unit will be clear of the village of ROUY'LE'GRAND by 5.30 a.m.

The Column will move in the following order:-
H.Q., No. 1 Section, No.2 Section, S.A.A.Section and 'B' Echelon and a destance of 200 yards between Sections.

The route to be taken will be as follows:-
MESNIL ST. NICAISE, MESNIL'LE'PETIT, POTTE, PERTAIN, OMIECOURT, CHAULNES, LIHONS, ROSIERES and CAIX.

H.Q. will move off from present lines at 3.30 a.m. and will proceed direct to MESNIL'LE'PETIT.

The Column will move off under the orders of Capt. P.N. Ludlow and will move off from MESNIL'LE'PETIT at 4.30 a.m. sharp.

R.Q.M.S. Spittle and the N.C.Os. or men detailed for billeting will report to 2/Lt. Daly at head of Column of 306th Art. Bde. at 5.40 a.m.

Sergt. Morris (H.Q) will report to 2/Lt. W.R. Page at the head of the Column of 306th Art. Bde.

2/Lt. G.H.Gibbs will report to the H.Q. 306th Art. Bde. at 7.0 p.m. tonight in order to synchronise watches and will be responsible that all Sections are in possession of Divisional time.

Section Commanders are reminded that they are personally responsible, as usual, that all billets and horse lines are left scrupulously clean and, if necessary, rear parties will be left behind.

Officers Commanding Sections will send a mounted man to report to the head of the Column at MESNIL'LE'PETIT as soon as they are ready to move.

The usual ten minutes to the hour halts will be taken and the time for the one hour halt for the purpose of watering will be notified from the head of the Column.

ACKNOWLEDGE.

Copy No. 1 War Diary.
" 2 Lieut.Col. F.W.Willock.
" 3 No. 1 Section.
" 4 No. 2 Section.
" 5 S.A.A.Section.
" 6 'B' Echelon.
" 7 Adjutant.

Captain & Adjutant
1st D.A.C.

Copy No. 1

appendix D

M A R C H   O R D E R S

for
21st May 1917
by
Lieut.Col. W. T. Cox,
Comdg. 61st Div. Ammn. Col.

Reference Map Amiens 17

H.Q. and all Sections will remain hooked in and ready to move at 5.15 a.m. care being taken to keep all main roads clear.

A cyclist orderly from H.Q. and a mounted man from each of the four Sections will report to the Adjutant at H.Q. Mess at 5 a.m.

As soon as the order is given to move, Sections will move in the same order as today and remain under the orders of Capt. P.H.Ludlow throughout the march.

The route for the D.A.C. is as follows:- WIENCOURT, MARCELCAVE, VILLERS BRETTONEUX to the Inn at Cross roads ½ mile South of BLANGY TRONVILLE where further orders will be received from the C.O. 306th Art. Bde. as to the exact route thereafter.

The billeting parties as detailed today, under the command of 2/Lt. Montgomery will leave D.A.C.H.Q. at 5.15 a.m. and will meet 2/Lt. Baly of 306th Art. Bde. at the Church BLANGY TRONVILLE at 8 a.m.

The Interpreter D.A.C. will report to 2/Lt. Baly at 306th Art. Bde. H.Q. at 5.15 a.m.

2/Lt. Pratt will report to 306th Art. Bde. H.Q. at 8 p.m. tonight to synchronise watches and will be responsible that all Units of the Column are in possession of Divisional time.

The usual ten minutes to the hour halts will be taken.

ACKNOWLEDGE.

Copy No. 1 War Diary
' 2 Lieut. Col. F.G.Willock.
' 3 No. 1 Section.
' 4 No. 2 Section.
' 5 S.A.A. Section
' 6 'B' Echelon.
' 7 Adjutant.

J.R. Aston
Captain & Adjutant,
61st D.A.C.

Appendix D E

COPY No:..1......

MARCHING ORDERS
for
22nd.May 1917.
by
LIEUT:COL:W.T.COX COMDG:61st.Div.Amm.Column.

Reference Maps ; AMIENS 17.1/100,000.
LENS 11. " "

The 61st.D.A.C.will move from the present area to NAOURS.

Headquarters,1 & 2 Sections will be drawn up ready to move at 6.a.m.,but must take care to keep all roads clear until the tail of the 306th.Brigade has cleared the X Roads ½ mile South of the "y" in GLISY.

Headquarters and "A"Echelon will then proceed by the same road namely;- The road leading from GLISY CHURCH to main AMIENS Rd., the head of the column moving under the orders of Capt.P.H. LUDLOW,at 6.a.m.

The S.A.A.Section and "B"Echelon will join the column on the main AMIENS Road by whichever road appears to the Section Comd'rs to be most convenient.

Route for all Units as follows;- Main road through LONGUEAU to AMIENS,turn to right at AMIENS STATION and follow the direct main road to FLESSELLES,thence to NAOURS.

The advance party under 2/Lieut.M.MONTGOMERY will leave D.A.C.HQ: at 5.15.a.m.,and will report to 2/Lieut.F.J.BALY at the TOWN MAJOR'S Office at "O"StreetNAOURS,at 8.45.a.m. (After entering NAOURS take RIGHT HAND ROAD at the first X Roads in the village.)
This office is about 300x on Left hand side of the street.

The Interpretor will report to 2/Lieut.F.J.BALY at 306th.Brigade Headquarters at 5.30.a.m.

Refilling Point 22nd.May 1917 HAVERNAS-CANAPLES Road near HAVERNAS-on arrival.

2/Lieut.BUCKETT will report at 306th.Brigade Headquarters at 7.p.m. tonight to synchronise watches,and will be responsible that HQ: D.A.C.,and all Sections are in possession of Divisional Time.

Wells at NAOURS for drinking purposes are plentiful and all marked with notice boards.

Sections will be prepared to march again on the 24th.inst:

The usual 10 minutes to the hour HALTS will be taken ,and also one hour for the purpose of water and feed which will be notified from the head of the column.

ACKNOWLEDGE.

[signature]
CAPT,
ADJUTANT,
61st.D.A.C.

Copy No.1.War Diary.
" " 2.Lt;Col;Willock.
" " 3.No.1.Section.
" " 4.No.2.Section.
" " 5. S.A.A.Section.
" " 6."B"Echelon.
" " 7. Adjutant.

Appendix F

Copy No. 1

MARCH ORDERS
for
24th May 1917
by
Lieut.Col.W.T.Cox
Cdg. 61st Divl. Ammn.Col.

Reference maps LENS 11

61st D. A. C. will move from the NAOURS area, H.Q. AND 'A' Echelon ~~and S.A.A. Section~~ to HEM. 'B' Echelon AND S.A.A. SECTION to HARDINVAL.

H.Q. will be at the cross roads TALMAS ready to move at 6 a.m. Care will be taken that all roads North of the Church are kept clear ~~of the Church~~ for 306th Art. Bde. Section Commanders will make their own arrangements for reaching the starting point and will do well to identify the best means of reaching the TALMAS road ~~tomorrow morning~~ tonight in order to avoid congestion with other Sections.

The Column will move in the usual order H.Q., No. 1 Section No. 2 Section S.A.A. Section and the mobile portion of 'B' Echelon.

Capt. P.H. Ludlow will take command of the Column.

The route to be taken is as follows:- LAVICOGNE, VERTGALAND FARM, BEAUVAL, GEZAINCOURT, BRETELto HEM.

An Advance party consisting of the Interpreter and the regular billeting party under command of 2/Lt. Montgomery will leave D.A.C. H.Q. Mess at 5.15 a.m. and will report at the office of the Town Major OCCOCHES where detailed instructions will be issued.

Refilling point will be on MEZEROLLES - DOULLENS road near OUTREBOIS on arrival.

Section Commanders will be responsible that all billets and horse lines in the NAOURS area are left scrupulously clean.

The wagons of 'B' Echelon which cannot be moved owing to shortage of animals will remain at NAOURS until the arrival of animals which will be sent back from HEM, subsequently rejoining the Column on the 26th instant.

The Supply Officer A.S.C. will if possible arrange to leave at NAOURS rations and forage for the 26th for this party ready for the arrival on evening of 25th. If these rations are not available the Supply Officer will so inform C.O. D.A.C. and a wagon will accompany the return party on 25th bringing rations and forage for the 26th.

Sections will obtain Divisional time from H.Q. office about 7 p.m. tonight.

Reference Daily Order of yesterday steel helmets will be worn by all ranks as soon as the Unit reaches the newarea.

The usual ten minutes to the hour halts will be taken.

Copy No. 1 War Diary
" 2 No. 1 Section
" 3 No. 2 Section
" 4 S.A.A.Section
" 5 'B' Echelon
" 6 Adjutant

[signature]
Captain & Adjutant,
61st D.A.C.

Confidential

Vol 14

War Diary

6th. Div. Am. Col.

Period 1st to 30th June 1917

Volume XIV

WAR DIARY
or
INTELLIGENCE SUMMARY.
(Erase heading not required.)

Army Form C. 2118.

Instructions regarding War Diaries and Intelligence Summaries are contained in F. S. Regs., Part II. and the Staff Manual respectively. Title pages will be prepared in manuscript.

Place	Date	Hour	Summary of Events and Information	Remarks and references to Appendices
Reference map LENS 11	1.6.17		HQ & A Echelon at HEM, B Echelon & S A A Section at BOISBERGUES, D B S between TILLOY-LEZ-MAFFLAINES & WANCOURT	
	"		49 O R arrived as re-inforcements from the Base, & were divided between 306 & 307 Art Bdes & D A C	
			the following being posted to D A C, 1 QMS, 2 Corpls, 1 Bdr, & 30 Gunners & Drivers	
	4.6.17		Lt Col W. T. COX Commanding 61 D A C appointed a member of the DISTINGUISHED SERVICE ORDER	(King's Birthday Honours)
	5.6.17		S A A Section inspected in Drill order by C.O at BOISBERGUES	
	7.6.17		Lt Col W T COX proceeded to ENGLAND on 10 Days Leave, Capt T R ALSTON assumed command of D A C	
	8.6.17	6.40am	61 D A C moved to LAHERLIERE via DOULLENS, POMMERA, MONDICOURT, SOLERNEAU & LARBRET	See [illegible]
	"		Capt T R ALSTON assumed command of the DIVISIONAL ARTILLERY & attached Units on the march	61 DIV ART ADMIN No 62
Reference map FRANCE 51B	9.6.17	3.0am	61 D A C moved from LAHERLIERE (SAULTY AREA) to ACHICOURT via BEAUMETZ-les-LOGES on ARRAS-DOULLENS RD.	
	"		Map References of new positions (HQ M 4 a 5 3) (No 1 M 4 b 2 5) (No 2 M 4 central) (S A A M 4 b 1 9) (B Echelon M 4 c 4 9) (DUMP M 4 c 2 5)	
	"		Lieut A S ALLEN appointed i/c DUMP assistant officer 2 Lt H K HAWSON	
	11.6.17		G O C R A 61 DIV inspected D A C Horse lines & DUMP	
	14.6.17		B S M TARPEY (B Echelon) appointed R S M, vice ~~2 Lt~~ RSM A G J CAMPBELL now serving as 2 Lieut in 35 D A C	
	14.6.17		Rev C H STAVELEY C.F reported to 61 D A C on attachment for duty with 61 DIV ART	
	"		37 mules received from No 18 Field Remount Station FREVENT & distributed amongst the Sections	
	19.6.17		2 Lt A THURLEY reported from the Base & was temporarily attached to S A A SECTION	

T2134. Wt. W708—776. 500000. 4/15. Sir J. C. & S.

Instructions regarding War Diaries and Intelligence Summaries are contained in F. S. Regs., Part II. and the Staff Manual respectively. Title pages will be prepared in manuscript.

WAR DIARY
or
INTELLIGENCE SUMMARY.
(Erase heading not required.)

Army Form C. 2118.

Place	Date	Hour	Summary of Events and Information	Remarks and references to Appendices
Reference Map FRANCE 51c				
	20.6.17		Lt Col W.T. COX DSO returned from leave & reassumed command of 61 DAC vice CAPT T R ALSTON	
	22.6.17		2Lt N.C. BARNES is attached from No 2 Section to SAA Section, 2Lt A THURLEY from SAA Section to No 2 Section, & is seconded for temporary duty at the D.A.C. Ammunition Dump. 2Lt H.K. HAWSON returned to SAA Section for duty & is relieved at the Dump by 2Lt A THURLEY	
	7.6.17		2Lt R.M. MONTGOMERY (B Echelon) is appointed orderly officer & attached to DAC H.Q	
	20.6.17		14 mules on loan to 183 Infy Bde for the move of the Division	2Lt H.G. ANSELL (B Echelon) proceeded in charge
	21.6.17		37 182 & 184 Infy Bde	
	19.6.17		DBS personnel returned from temporary attachment to the Division at WARLUS, & were attached to the B Echelon for duty at the AMMUNITION DUMP. 2Lt C R LEEKE remains with Divisional HQ	
	19.6.17		2Lt A THURLEY reported from Base and posted to S.A.A	WTC
	25.6.17		2Lt H.G. ANSELL returned with personnel and animals loaned to Infantry Brigades	WTC
	27.6.17	8am	61st DAC moved to HABARCQ via ACHICOURT, DAINVILLE, WARLUS & MONTENESCOURT.	WTC
	29.6.17		Capt T R ALSTON, Adjutant proceeded on special leave	WTC

W.T. Cox
Lieut. Colonel, R.F.A.
Commanding 61st (S.M.) Div. Amn. Col.

T2134. Wt. W708–776. 500000. 4/15. Sir J. C. & S.

Vol 15

Confidential

War. Diary

6th. D. A. C

Period. 1st to 31st July 1917

VOL. XV.

Instructions regarding War Diaries and Intelligence Summaries are contained in F. S. Regs., Part II. and the Staff Manual respectively. Title pages will be prepared in manuscript.

WAR DIARY
or
INTELLIGENCE SUMMARY.
(Erase heading not required.)

Army Form C. 2118.

Place	Date	Hour	Summary of Events and Information	Remarks and references to Appendices
Reference Map LENS 11 1:100,000	1.7.17		61 D.A.C in rest at HABARCQ	
"	4.7.17		1 L.D Horse & 39 mules received from No. 2 advanced Depot ABBEVILLE & were divided as follows No. 1 No. 2 & B Echelon 10 mules each, SAA Section 1 L.D Horse & 9 mules.	
"	1.7.17–7.7.17		Sections – Normal Routine	
"	8.7.17	4.40 am	61 D.A.C moved from HABARCQ to REBREUVIETTE, Route as follows – HABARCQ, NOYELLETTE, AVESNES LE COMTE, LIENCOURT LE CAUROY, ETRÉE-WAMIN, WAMIN, ROZIÈRE. (Appendix A)	
	9.7.17	5.30 am	61 D.A.C moved from REBREUVIETTE to CROIX, Route as follows – REBREUVIETTE, REBREUVE, GRAND BOURET FRÉVENT, NUNCQ, ECOIVRES, CROISETTE, SIRACOURT, CROIX (Appendix B)	
LENS 11	10.7.17		61 D.A.C rested at CROIX	
HAZEBROUCK 5a	11.7.17	5.30 am (Appendix C)	61 D.A.C moved from CROIX to NÉDONCHELLE & NÉDON Route as follows CROIX, PIERREMONT, LIBESSART, FLEURY, ANVIN, BERGUENEUSE, HEUCHIN, FONTAINE-lez-BOULANS, PALFART, FONTAINE-lez-HERMANS, NÉDONCHELLE NÉDON	
"	12.7.17	5.26 am	61 D.A.C moved from NÉDON (A Echelon) & NÉDONCHELLE (SAA HQ & B Echelon) to THIENNES (HQ) PECQUEUR (SAA) & NEUFPRÉ (A Echelon & B Echelon) – Route as follows AMETTES, BELLERY, AMES, LIÈRES, ST. HILAIRE, NORRENT FONTES, FONTES WALLON CAPPEL, MAZINGHEM, LAMBRES & AIRE (Appendix D)	
"	13.7.17	4.30 am	61 D.A.C moved from AIRE AREA to STAPLE & OXELAERE AREA via main PECQUEUR – OXELAERE road through [illegible] E A draft of 3 N.C.Os 20 Drivers 21 gunners & 6 Signallers arrived from RH & R.F.A Base Depot & were distributed between the 2 Bdes & D.A.C.	

T2134. Wt. W708–776. 500000. 4/15. Sir J. C. & S.

Instructions regarding War Diaries and Intelligence Summaries are contained in F. S. Regs., Part II. and the Staff Manual respectively. Title pages will be prepared in manuscript.

WAR DIARY
or
INTELLIGENCE SUMMARY.
(Erase heading not required.)

Army Form C. 2118.

Place	Date	Hour	Summary of Events and Information	Remarks and references to Appendices
HAZEBROUCK 5a				
"	14.7.17	4.25 am	61 D.A.C moved from OXELAERE AREA to EECKE AREA via OXELAERE, outskirts of CASSEL HAUTE ROME and STEENVOORDE	Appendix F
BELGIUM & FRANCE Sheet 27 N.E Scale 1:20,000	15.7.17	10.3	61 D.A.C moved from EECKE AREA to WINNEZEELE AREA via STEENVOORDE, ST LAURENT & DROOGLANDT	Appendix G
			Map References of D.A.C HQ & 4 Sections { H.Q K.2.c 0.6. No 1 K.2.b 4.0 No 2 K.2.b 4.0 } SAA K.2.c 3.3. Bachelor K.1.d 4.1.	
"	20.7.17		Inspection of all Sections & Headquarters in full marching order by G.O.C R.A accompanied by Brigade Major R.A	
"	16.7.17		30 O.R from A & B Echelons attached for duty in the line with 15th Divisional Artillery	
"	23.7.17		1 officer (2Lt H.G. ANSELL) & 35 O.R. relieved above 30 men	
"	24.7.17		1 Farrier Sergt & 22 O.R proceeded under the command of Major W.H TAYLOR as part of a Collecting party to draw remounts from No 5 Base Remount Depot CALAIS	
"	"		Exchange of personnel for a fortnight's training, between 306 Art Bde & D.A.C 2 officers 1 Sergt 1 Corpl 2 Bombadiers & 20 O.R. D.A.C officers { 2Lt F.J. PRATT 2Lt M.C. PERROTT } 306 Bde officers { 2Lt LAXTON 2Lt FALLON }	attached LAXTON No 1 FALLON No 2
"	26.7.17		2Lt H.G ANSELL & 33 O.R returned from attachment to 15 Divisional Arty	
"	27.7.17		36 mules received from No 5 Base Remount Depot CALAIS	
"	"		Draft of 46 O.R arrived from Base Depot HAVRE	
"	"		Exchange of personnel for a fortnight's training between 307 Art Bde & D.A.C 2 officers 1 Sergt 1 Corpl 2 Bombadiers & 20 O.R D.A.C officers { 2Lt R.G.B. CHASE 2Lt BUCKETT } 307 Bde officers { }	

Instructions regarding War Diaries and Intelligence Summaries are contained in F. S. Regs., Part II. and the Staff Manual respectively. Title pages will be prepared in manuscript.

WAR DIARY
or
INTELLIGENCE SUMMARY.
(Erase heading not required.)

Army Form C. 2118.

Place	Date	Hour	Summary of Events and Information	Remarks and references to Appendices
BELGIUM & FRANCE Sheet 27 NE.	26.7.17		Adjutant proceeded with Staff Capt. R.A. to inspect ground alloted to unit in Forward	area I
"	27.7.17		Adjutant took forward 4 Section Commanders & R.S.M. to inspect new area between BRANDHOEK & VLAMERTINGHE (Reference map BELGIUM Sheet 28 N.W. Edition 6A scale 1/20,000 H 7.	I 8.13.14 Central
BELGIUM Sheet 28 N.W.	31.7.17	6.20 am.	61 D.A.C moved from WINNEZEELE AREA to Forward AREA (H 7.8.13 14 Central) Route as follows - DROGLANDT, STEENVOORDE, BEAUVOORDE, ABEELE, POPERINGHE, BRANDHOEK	(appendix H)

31:7:17

I. R. Aston
Capt & Adjt
for Lieut. Colonel, R.F.A.
Commanding 61st (S.M.) Div. Amm. Col.

T2134. Wt. W708—776. 500000. 4/15. Sir J. C. & S.

Copy No 2

Appendix A

March Order

by

Lieut. Col. W. T. Cox D.S.O.
Commanding 61st Div. Am. Col.

Ref. Map. LENS. 11

1. The 61st D.A.C. will move from its present station tomorrow morning, Sunday, 8th instant in the following order: HQ, No 1 Section, No 2 Section, S.A.A. Section, 'B' Echelon.

2. Starting point, Cross roads at HABARCQ CHATEAU. H.Q. will be at the starting point ready to move at 4.30 am. and No 1 Section will as far as possible pull out on to the road in rear

3. A distance of 500 yards will be maintained between each Section.

4. Capt P.H. LUDLOW will be in charge of the Column.

5. The route to be taken is as follows:- AVESNES-LE-COMTE, LIENCOURT, ETREE WAMIN, WAMIN, ROZIERE, to REBREUVIETTE.

6. Billeting party consisting of the Interpreter, 2/Lt R.M. Montgomery, R.Q.M.S. Spittle and one N.C.O. from each Section with necessary horseholders will proceed to the REBREUVIETTE area today. They will report to 2/Lt Montgomery at DACHQ at 5 pm this evening. Feeds and rations will be carried.

7. Watering. There is an insufficiency of troughs and fords and buckets baskets will be required. Water will be drawn from the river.

8. Section guides will be at the A in STA. on the WAMIN-SAUROY road at 10 am to guide supply wagons. Refilling point at same place at 3pm.

9. Horse lines and billets will be left scrupulously clean and the usual rear parties will be detailed to burn or bury all refuse, paper, tins &c. Section Commanders are reminded that they are entirely responsible that the area is left in a satisfactory condition. All latrines, cookhouses, billets and horse lines &c will be inspected by an officer of each Section and before the Unit leaves a report will be rendered to this office stating that this has been carried out, and that everything is in order.

10. Guides for supply wagons will accompany the billeting party

11. Baggage wagons will report to Sections at 6 pm tonight 7th instant

12. Section Commanders are warned to see that the turnout of their men, animals and wagons is as good as possible as the GOCRA will in all probability, inspect the DAC as it passes his HQrs.

13. Nosebags will be carried filled and as high up on the saddle as possible with the mess tin on left side of nosebag. It was noticed that in only one Section was the equipment correctly carried when the Column moved from its last battle station.

14. Steel helmets will not be worn but carried under the left shoulder strap.

15. The usual 10 minute halts will be taken; the first at 5.50 am

16. An officer from each Section will report at H.Q. office at 7pm tonight to synchronise watches.

ACKNOWLEDGE.

Copy No 1 to C.O
" " 2 " War Diary.
" " 3 " O/C No 1 Section
" " 4 " O/C No 2 Section
" " 5 " O/C S.A.A. Section
" " 6 " O/C 'B' Echelon.
" " 7 " R.S.M. Tarpey.

W. T. Cox

Copy No 2

March Orders
by
Lt. Col. W. T. Cox. D.S.O
Commdg. 61st Div. Ammn. Col.

Ref. Map. LENS. 11. 1/100,000.

1. 61st D.A.C. will move from its present station to CROIX on 9th instant.

2. Starting point road junction 900 yard S.W. of the first R in REBREUVE.

3. The Column will move under the command of Capt P. H. LUDLOW. in the same order as today

4. Headqrs. will be at the starting point at 5.15 am and Sections will arrange to be clear of their parks so that the head of the Column may move at 5.30 am. sharp. maintaining a distance of 500 yards between Sections.

5. Route to be taken is as follows:- GRAND BOURET FREVENT, NUNCQ, ECOIVRES, CROISETTE, SIRACOURT.

6. Billeting party constituted as today will leave H.Q at 5 am

7. Guides for ASC wagons will accompany the advance party and will be at S in STA on the HERLIN LE SEC - ST POL road at 9 am. Refilling point on the 9th and 10th at junction of the CROIX road with the GAUCHIN - WAVRANS road at 3 pm

8. Water at ford 1½ miles E of CROIX. In order to facilitate watering as many horses of 306 Bde as possible should be E of the river TERNOISE and DAC will use the W bank of the river at the ford.

9. Wagons will be parked on the sides of the CROIX - ST POL road. Horses in the avenue leading to the Chateau

10. The march will not be resumed until July 11th

11. An officer from each Section will report at HQ (at Chateau) before 9.30 pm. tonight to synchronize watches

12. Section Commanders will issue all necessary orders for leaving the billeting area in a satisfactory condition and rear parties will be left where necessary

13. The usual 10 minute halts will be taken the first at 6-50 a

ACKNOWLEDGE.

Copy No 1	Comdg. Officer	
" " 2.	War Diary	
" " 3	O/C No 1 Section	
" " 4	" " 2 "	
" " 5	" S.A.A. "	
" " 6.	" 'B' Echelon	
" " 7	R.S.M.	

[signature]
Capt & Adjt.
61 D.A.C.

8.55 pm.

Copy No 7

Appendix C

March Order
by
Lt. Colonel W T Cox DSO
Comdg. 61st. Div Ammn. Column

Ref Map LENS 11.
HAZEBROUCK Sheet 5a

1. The 61st DAC will move from its present station to NEDON tomorrow 11th inst.

2. Starting Point Cross Roads, PIERRE MONT - BEAUVOIS - CROIX - HUMIERES.

3. The Column will move from the starting point under the orders of Captain P.H. Ludlow at 5.30 a.m.

4. The route to be taken is as follows:- PIERREMONT, LIBESSART FLEURY, ANVIN, BERGUENEUSE, HEUCHIN, FONTAINE-LEZ-BOULANS, FONTAINE-LEZ-HERMANS, NEDONCHELLE.

5. The Column will move in the same order as before, Headquarters leading

6. Billeting Party constituted as before will leave H.Q. Chateau at 5.0 a.m.

7. Guides for Supply wagons will accompany the billeting party & will meet the supply wagons on the FERFAY - AUCHY road at bridge at BELLERY at 10.0 am. Refilling point on high ground on BELLERY-FERFAY road at 3.0 pm.

8. Watering in troughs in village of NEDON. All village pumps will be found to be in working order.

9. An Officer from each Section will report at H.Q. Office at 5.0 pm today to synchronise watches.

10. Owing to the change in the route to be taken the wagons will be found to be pointing the wrong way, i.e. towards ST POL. It is left to the discretion of Sections Commanders as to whether the wagons are turned during daylight today

11. Horse Lines & Billets will, as usual be left scrupulously clean & rear parties left where necessary

12. The usual 10 minute halts will be taken, the first at 6.50 am.

ACKNOWLEDGE

Copy No 1 Comdg Officer
" " 2 War Diary
" 3 No 1. Section
" 4 " 2
" 5 SAA Section
" 6 B Echelon
" 7 R.S.M.

W. T. Cox
Lieut Colonel
Commanding 61. DAC

Copy No 2

March Orders
by
Lt Col. W.T. Cox. D.S.O
Comdg. 61st D. A. Column.

Ref. Map. HAZEBROUCK 5a 1/100,000

1. The 61st DAC. will move from present station to NEUFPRÉ and PECQUEUR. tomorrow 12th instant

2. The Column will move under the orders of Capt. R. H. LUDLOW in the same order as today.

3. Starting point will be at the Cross roads 1000 yds E of NEDON Church

4. Time of starting 5. 25 am

5. Route to be taken is as follows:- AMETTES, BELLERY, AMES, LIERES, St. HILAIRE, FONTES, MAZINGHEM, LAMBRES, AIRE.

6. Sections will be billeted as follows. 'A' and 'B' Echelons at NEUFPRÉ, HQs and S.A.A. Section at PECQUEUR.

7. Advance billeting party constituted as today will leave NEDON church at 4.30 am.

8. Guides for supply wagons will accompany the advance party and will be at St. MARTIN, N of AIRE-THEROUANNE railway at 10 am. Refilling point same place at 10 am.

9. Watering for the Unit in troughs at NEUFPRÉ

10. An officer from each Section will report to Brigade office at 6pm to synchronise watches.

11. The usual 10 minute halts will be taken, the first at 5. 5_0 am

12. Section Commanders are reminded that horse lines and wagon parks should be left clean and rear parties left where necessary

13. Sections will render to HQ. office as soon as possible after arrival in new area, a list of all billets occupied.

This order holds good for the rest of the trek

ACKNOWLEDGE.

Copy.
No 1 Cdg. Officer.
No 2 War Diary
No 3 O/C No 1 Section
No 4 " 2 "
No 5 " S.A.A "
No 6 " 'B' Echelon
No 7. R S. M.

Issued 5. 15 pm

[signature]
Capt & Adj.
61 DAC.

COPY No 2

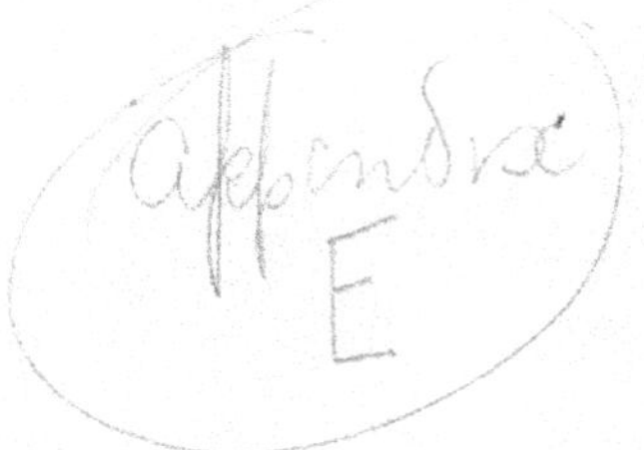

March Orders
by
Lt. Col. W. T. Cox. D.S.O.
Comdg. 61st D. A. C.

Reference Map. HAZEBROUCK. 5a.

1. The 61st D. A. C. will move from present station to area midway between STAPLE and OXELAERE tomorrow 18th instant.

2. The Column will move under the orders of Capt P. H. LUDLOW in the same order as today.

3. Starting point road junction 1400x W of THIENNES Station (road junction is just N of PECQUEUR LOCK with field of mustard at road corner). Starting time 4.30 am.

4. Route to be taken is as follows:- just E of STEENBECQUE, HALLONCAPPEL.

5. The arrangements for the advanced billeting party and guides are altered for tomorrows march. One Officer per Section, Q.M.S and horse holder will leave the starting point as detailed above at 4 ~~[illegible]~~ am. Billets for Sections are allocated as follows

No	NAME	MAP REF	Off.	O.R.	Section
101	BERQUIN	O. 29. B. 0. 8	2	100	No 1
102	HELLAERT	O. 29. C. 7. 1	3	100	No1, 50 — No 2, 50
103	LEROY	O. 35 a 5. 6	6	100	No 2.
104	DEGUIOT	O. 35 c. 3. 4	4	150	S.A.A.
105	MORRIAUX	O. 35 B 6. 7	6	250.	H.Q. 50 'B' Ech 200

Horses will as far as possible be equally divided between all farms. 15 Officers billets are available in Nos 101 to 104 and must be mutually divided between Sections. The 6 officers billets at 105 are required for H.Q.

6. Q.M.Ss will return to LONGUE CROIX U. 5. C. 3. 4 to guide Sections to billets.

7. Guides for supply wagons will accompany the billeting party and will be at STAPLEMARKET at 10am. Refilling point, same time and place.

8. Care will be taken that billets are left scrupulously clean and rear parties left where necessary.

9. An officer from each Section will report at ~~each~~ H.Q. at 6 pm to synchronize watches.

10. Owing to the large number of troops moving, Units will occupy only the billets which are allocated to them in the STAPLE - BECKE district.

11. In these two districts in the 2nd Army area a certificate will be furnished by Sections that all pumps troughs, tents, cookhouses and latrine fittings, shewn in the area occupied by them, are left in position and in good order. Any stores broken or deficient should be noted.

12. The usual 10 minute halts will be taken the first at 5.50 am

ACKNOWLEDGE

[signature]
Capt & Adjt.
61 D.A.C.

Copy No 1 Cdg. Off.
" 2. War Diary
" 3 O/C. No 1 Section
" 4 " 2 "
" 5 " S.A.A. "
" 6. " 'B' Echelon
" 7. R. S. M.

Copy No 2

March Orders
by
Lt Col Wm T Cox D.S.A.
Comdg 61st D.A. Column

* and 2 pumps at Q4.04.6
on Farm 416

Reference maps HAZEBROUCK 5a
FRANCE Sh 27SW
" " 27SE
" 27NE

1 The 61 DAC will move from present station to area S of STEENVOORDE - BEAUVOORDE road tomorrow 14th

2 The Column will move in the same order as today under the command of Capt P.H. HURNOW.

3 Starting point, road junction 500x S of the O in OXELAERE. Time, 4.30am

4 The route to be taken will be as follows OXELAERE, outskirts of CASSEL, HAUTEROME, STEENVOORDE.

5 Advance party constituted as today under the comnd of the Orderly Officer will leave the starting point at 4 am. Guides will be at the CASSEL entrance of STEENVOORDE not later than 6.45 am to guide the sections to their wagon lines

6 Guides for supply wagons will accompany the advance party. R filling point ~~and place for guide to report will be notified later~~ Market Place at STEENVOORDE at 10 ams.

7 The following list are the only billets available for the Unit in the new area and tents and trench shelters will have to be used to make up for lack of accomodation.

BILLET No	NAME	MAP REF	OFFs	O.R.	HORSES	SECTION
418	Staelen	Q.4.B.3.6.	3	150} 100}	446	No 1
419	Mussian	Q.4.C.8.7.	1	15		S.A.A.
420	Minne	Q.4.B.6.2		15	-	S.A.A.
421	Heyman	Q.5.A.5.5		50	-	H.Q.
423	Maeseneesen	K.35.C.2.4		{75 {75	-	No 2 'B' Ech.
424	Charly	Q.4.B.9.9		30	-	No 2
425	Verhaeghe	Q.3.B.7.7		30	-	S.A.A.
* in fields	Q.4.C.0.4 and Q.4.C.3.6			{75 {75	* 446	No 2 'B' Ech

8 Watering arrangements, four 400 gallon troughs * (2 sides) Water pumped from pond on farm.

9 Special steps will be taken to see that all horses are securely picketed to prevent damage to crops and all gates to fields in which horses are picketted will be kept closed.

10 Section Commanders will see that all horse lines & billets in the OXELAERE area are left scrupulously clean.

11 The first halt will be held at 5.50a.

12 An officer from each Section will report to the Orderly Officer at HQ at 7.0pm this evening to synchronise watches

13 The Unit will be prepared to move again on the 15th

14 One man from each Section, carrying rations for 2 days will report dismounted to RQMS Spittle at SAA Section billet No 104 at 5am. (Men are required as advance party for final area.

ACKNOWLEDGE

Copy No 1 Cdg. Officer
" " 2 War Diary
" " 3 O/C No 1 Section
" " 4 " 2
" " 5 " SAA
" " 6 " B Echelon
" " 7 RSM

Issued at 5.5.

[signature] Capt & Adjt 61 DAC

Copy No 2.

March Orders by Lt. Col. W. T. COX. D.S.O Comdg. 61st D. A. Col. for 15th July 1917

Ref Maps. BELGUIM & FRANCE
27 SE & 27 N.E 1/20000

1/ The D.A.C. will move from present station to the WINNEZEELE area, tomorrow July 15th.

2/ The Column will move under the orders of Lt Col. W.T. COX D.S.O.

3/ Starting point road junction Q.3 D.5.1. Time 10.3 am

4/ Route to be taken is as follows, STEENVOORDE, ST LAURENT, DROGLANDT.

5/ 61 D.A. Order No 71 and 61 D.A. No BMS/2/41, copy of which letters are forwarded herewith to each Section should be carefully read and carried out to the letter.

6/ The advance billeting parties from Sections after having received instructions from the Adjt tonight will proceed under the orders of their own Section Commanders, at times to be chosen by them, to the new area in advance of the Column

7 Guides will meet the Column at DROGLANDT. J.12.B.8.6 to guide Sections to ~~their wagon~~ lines

8/ The EECKE area will as usual be left scrupulously clean

9 Section Commanders should arrange mutually tonight as to the best means of clearing their parks so as to avoid the slightest delay at the starting point tomorrow morning.

10/ An officer from each Section will report to the Orderly Officer at Bde H.Q at 8.30 am tomorrow morning to synchronise watches.

ACKNOWLEDGE.

Issued at 6.45 pm

Copy No	1	Cdg Officer
"	2	War Diary
"	3	O/C No 1 Section
"	4	" 2 "
"	5	S A A
"	6	B Echelon
"	7	R.S.M

[signature]
Capt & Adjt
61 DAC

Copy No 8

Marching Orders
for Tuesday July 31st 1917.
by
Lieut-Colonel W.T. Cox D.S.O.
Commanding 61st Divisional Amm^n Column

Appendix
11

Reference Maps
BELGIUM & FRANCE No 27 & 28

1/ The 61st D.A.C. will move from present station to new area tomorrow morning 31st inst.

2/ The Column will move under the orders of the C.O. Capt. P.H. Ludlow will ride at the head of the Column.

3/ Starting point road junction J.12. b.8.7 (DROGLANDT) time 6.20. am.

4/ Route to be taken will be as follows STEENVOORDE. cross roads K.35.d. ABEELE, POPERINGHE, BRANDHOEK cross roads H.7.c.3.5.

5/ The actual area to be occupied by Sections has already been shown to Section Commanders

*6/ Advanced party consisting of Lieut R.M. Montgomery RSM. Tarfey & 1 N.C.O. from each Section with necessary horse-holders will leave H.Q. at 6.0. am. & proceed to the new area by the shortest route.

7/ The usual distance of 500 yards will be kept between Sections.

8/ The greatest secrecy will be maintained & on no account will the move or time of departure be mentioned in the hearing of civilian inhabitants. This fact is to be impressed on your Sergeant Major & office staff.

9/ The usual 10 minutes halts will be taken the first at 6.50. am.

10/ All area stores will be dumped at H.Q. & handed over to Cpl Best ~~at~~ either before the Sections move or as soon afterwards as possible. A certificate as to the amount which is being handed over signed by the Section Commander will be in this office by 7.30. pm this evening

11/ The area will as usual be left scrupulously clean.

12/ Section Commanders will detail an officer to report to H.Q. office at 8.0. pm. tonight in order to synchronise watches.

13/ Steel Helmets & Box-respirators in the 'alert' position will be worn by all ranks

*14/ Para 6 above is cancelled. The advance party will accompany the Column as far as POPERINGHE & will then ride forward.

Copy No 1 - C.O.
2 - Adjt.
3 - O.C. No 1 Sect.
4 - " 2 "
5 - " S.A.A. "

Copy No 6 - O.C. 'B' Ech.
" 7 - RSM.
" 8 - War Diary

[signature]
Capt & Adjt
61 D.A.C.

Confidential

War Diary

61st Div Am Col.

Period 1-31 Aug 17

Vol 16

Instructions regarding War Diaries and Intelligence Summaries are contained in F. S. Regs., Part II. and the Staff Manual respectively. Title pages will be prepared in manuscript.

WAR DIARY
or
INTELLIGENCE SUMMARY.
(Erase heading not required.)

Army Form C. 2118.

Place	Date	Hour	Summary of Events and Information	Remarks and references to Appendices
Reference map BELGIUM Sheet 28 N.W.	1:8:17		Position of 61 D.A.C H 7.8:13.14 Central (South BRANDHOEK AREA)	
" "	2:8:17		61 D.A.C moves to VLAMERTINGHE AREA (H.8.9 Central map Reference of H.Q (H.9.C 1.3½)	
" "	5:8:17		61 D.A.C came under orders of 36 D.A.C for ammunition supply	
" "			Party of 4 officers & 80 men took over 2 forward ammunition Dumps, PICKERING (I.2.a.9½.6) & OVERTON (I.2.d 8.6)	
" "	6:8:17		Draft of 58 Horses collected from PROVEN by Lt R.M. MONTGOMERY for 61 DIV. ART. (20 Horses allotted to Sections of D.A.C)	
" "	8:8:17		CAPT T.R. ALSTON reported for duty to 36 DIV as assistant Staff Capt R.A., duties of adjutant 61 D.A.C. performed by the Commanding officer	
" "	7:8:17		Draft of 2 Drivers arrived from the Base, both men detailed to 306 Art Bde.	
" "	10 8 17		3 L D horses received from PROVEN	M.C.
" "	12 8 17		2Lt M C Perrott returned from 306th Brigade	M.C.
" "	13 8 17		1 Officers charger received from 307th Brigade on reorganisation of ride horses of Div Arts	M.C.
	"		2Lt H P R Coveney wounded at OVERTON DUMP and admitted to hospital	M.C.
" "	14 8 17		Lt H P R Coveney ~~and~~ 2Lt E S L Webb & 2Lt J de Lanbenque reported for duty from 9th Div Art	M.C.
" "	16 8 17		2Lt A H Thompson & 2Lt H Baker reported for duty from 9th Div Art	M.C.
" "	14 8 17		2Lt F J E Pratt returned from 306th Bde	

T2134. Wt. W708–776. 500000. 4/15. Sir J. C. & S.

Instructions regarding War Diaries and Intelligence Summaries are contained in F. S. Regs., Part II. and the Staff Manual respectively. Title pages will be prepared in manuscript.

WAR DIARY
or
INTELLIGENCE SUMMARY.
(Erase heading not required.)

Army Form C. 2118.

Place	Date	Hour	Summary of Events and Information	Remarks and references to Appendices
	14.8.17		2Lt J Baker proceeded to forward dump to relieve 2Lt A J Thompson	MC
	15.8.17		Lt R G B Chase proceeded to forward dump to relieve Lt G J Gibbs	MC
	"		2Lt A J Thompson was transferred to Trench Mortars	MC
	"		15 gunners were posted to 307th Brigade to replace casualties	MC
	"		HQs moved to H.9.a.0.0.	MC
	16.8.17		2Lt M C Perrott and 2Lt F J E Pratt transferred to 306th Brigade	MC
	17.8.17		Lieut J T James proceeded to forward dump to relieve 2Lt J de Lanbengue	MC
	"		2Lt J de Lanbengue transferred to Trench Mortars	MC
	"		Draft of 1 Cpl. 1 Bdr & 6 OR arrived from Base. Cpl & 6 OR posted to 307th Bde & Bdr to T. Ms	MC
	23.8.17		55th DAC relieved 36th Div A C and took over the supply of ammunition	MC
	24.8.17		9 OR arrived from Corps Rest Station and were sent to 307th Bde.	MC
	"		1 Cpl & 17 OR arrived from base and were posted as follows:- Cpl & 12 to 306, 4 men 307 Bde & 1 man DAC	MC
	25.8.17		Lt G. Knowles & 86 OR arrived from base and were posted as follows:- Officer & 20 OR to DAC, 46 OR to T.Ms 10 OR to 306 Bde & 10 OR to 307 Bde	MC
	26.8.17		6 OR arrived from base and posted, 4 to 307th Bde & 2 to 306 Bde.	MC
	28.8.17		DAC personnel at OVERTON DUMP relieved by 55th DAC	MC
	"		40 men under 2Lt E S L Webb & 2Lt H G Ansell proceeded to STANLEY DUMP to relieve party from 55th DAC	MC

T2134. Wt. W708–776. 500000. 4/15. Sir J. C. & S.

Instructions regarding War Diaries and Intelligence Summaries are contained in F. S. Regs., Part II. and the Staff Manual respectively. Title pages will be prepared in manuscript.

WAR DIARY
or
INTELLIGENCE SUMMARY.
(Erase heading not required.)

Army Form C. 2118.

Place	Date	Hour	Summary of Events and Information	Remarks and references to Appendices
	30.8.17		2/Lt J Buckett and Lt Geo Knowles proceeded to 307th Bde.	[initials]
	31.8.17		DAC personnel at PICKERING DUMP relieved by 55th DAC	[initials]
	"		2 Sgts, 3 Cpls, 3 Bdrs, and 25 OR proceed to STANLEY DUMP	[initials]
	"		14 signallers reported from Base	[initials]
	"		2/Lt C A Thurley reported from Base and posted to No 2 Section	[initials]
	"		10 LD horses received from Mob. Vet. Section & allocated as follows 4 to No 1 Sec, 3 to No 2 Sec, 3 to 'B' Echelon	[initials]

[signature]
Lieut. Colonel. R.F.A.
Commanding 61st (S.M.) Div. Amn. Col.

T2131. Wt. W708—776. 500000. 4/15. Sir J. C. & S.

Confidential

War Diary

61st DAC

1st to 30th Sept 1917

Vol XVII

Instructions regarding War Diaries and Intelligence Summaries are contained in F. S. Regs., Part II. and the Staff Manual respectively. Title pages will be prepared in manuscript.

WAR DIARY
or
INTELLIGENCE SUMMARY.
(*Erase heading not required.*)

Army Form C. 2118.

Place	Date	Hour	Summary of Events and Information	Remarks and references to Appendices
VLAMERTINGHE AREA	2:9:17		2nd Lt N.C. BARNES posted to XIX Corps Amm. Park	
" "	3:9:17		2 Lt E.S.L. Webb posted to 306 Art. Bde	
" "	2:9:17		5 O.R arrived from the Base & were posted to 306 Art Bde	
" "	3:9:17		40 mules collected from PROVEN & were distributed between "A" & "B" Echelons	
" "	9:9:17		26 O.R arrived from the Base & were posted as follows (11 306 Art Bde, 1 150 " ", 14 D.A.C)	
" "	10:9:17		12 " " " No 2 Reinforcement Coy 4 men posted to each Section	
" "	11:9:17		30 " " " the Base & were posted as follows (1 Trench mortars, 14 306 Art Bde, 15 307 Art Bde)	
" "	12:9:17		2 NCO & 21 men reported for duty at STANLEY DUMP in relief of 5 9" T M's	
" "	"		R.S.M. Tarpey & R.Q.M.S. Spittle were both buried in their dug out as a result of hostile shelling. R.S.M. Tarpey killed instantaneously, R.Q.M.S. Spittle died within a few minutes after being dug out. Both NCO's were buried in VLAMERTINGHE Cemetery	13:9:17
" "	"		Lt Col W.T. COX D.S.O. admitted to CORPS REST STATION with shell shock	
" "	13:9:17		CAPT I.R. ALSTON assumed command of 61 D.A.C during illness of Lt Col W.T. COX DSO	
" "	16:9:17		4 Rides & 42 L.D. horses collected from PROVEN & were distributed in the Unit	
" "	17:9:17	7.50 am	61 D.A.C moved to WATOU Artillery AREA via VLAMERTINGHE – POPERINGHE Rd, North SWITCH Road, ST JAN-TER-BIEZEN, WATOU. Reference map B.E.F sheet 27 N.E. HQ K.2.c.0.6, S.A.A K.2.c.3.3, No 1 K.3.c.2.9, B Echelon K.1.d.3.1, No 2 K.2.b.4.0	

T2134. Wt. W708–776. 500000. 4/15. Sir J. C. & S.

Instructions regarding War Diaries and Intelligence Summaries are contained in F. S. Regs., Part II. and the Staff Manual respectively. Title pages will be prepared in manuscript.

WAR DIARY
or
INTELLIGENCE SUMMARY.
(Erase heading not required.)

Army Form C. 2118.

Place	Date	Hour	Summary of Events and Information	Remarks and references to Appendices
WATOU Arty AREA	18:9:17		44 Remounts collected from PROVEN and distributed as follows: 306 Art Bde – 14; 307 – 15; D.A.C – 15	
"	21:9:17	5.15 am	Advanced Billeting party under command of Lt A. J. PYLE left POPERINGHE by train to MAREUIL	Appendix B
"	22.9.17	12.30 pm	Proceedings of a Field General C.M. held for the trial of No 88928 Dr CASTLE H.W. No 2 Section duly promulgated	
"	22/23		Headquarters, SAA Section, B Echelon moved from the WATOU ARTY AREA proceeding by Road to GODWAERSVELDE (in accordance with attached orders marked Appendix A) ENTRAINING STATION – GODWAERSVELDE; DETRAINING STATION – ARRAS	
"	23:9:17		No 1 Section attached to 306 Art Bde, moved from WATOU ARTY AREA: Entraining Station HOPOUTRE, Detraining Station ARRAS; No 2 Section " 307: Entraining Station PROVEN, Detraining Station AUBIGNY	Appendix C
St CATHERINE ARRAS	23/24		61 D.A.C re-assembled in new area Reference map FRANCE 51B (G.13.b)	
WATOU A.A.	22.9.18		2 officers & 38 O R from 61 Trench mortars attached to 61 D.A.C for the move	
"	"		Lt Col W.T. COX D.S.O. evacuated from No 62 C.C.S HARINGHE to the BASE	
St CATHERINE ARRAS	27:9:18		The following Reliefs were carried out at 10 am: [ANZIN DUMP No 1] Lt H.K HAWSON, 1 Sergt, 1 Cpl/Bomb. & 3 men (S.A.A. Section) relieved like party of 17 D.A.C	
"			LARESSET DUMP (near AGNEZ-les-DUISANS) 1 N.C.O. & 3 men (B Echelon) } relieving personnel of 17 D.A.C	
"			HORSESHOE DUMP (near DAINVILLE) 1 officer (Lt J.T. JAMES) } relieving personnel of 17 D.A.C	
	30:9:18		Re-organization of D.A.C. begun	
	29:9:18		Lt A.E. ALLEN relieved Lt J.T. JAMES at HORSESHOE DUMP	

[signature] Capt
Comdg 61 D.A.C.

T2134. Wt. W708–776. 500000. 4/15. Sir J. C. & S.

War Diary Appendix A

COPY №. 4

March Orders
for HQ, S.A.A. Sect & 'B' Echelon D.A.C.
by
Capt. T.R. ALSTON
Commanding 61 Divisional Ammn Column.

1. Headquarters, SAA Section & 'B' Echelon will be ready to move any time after midnight on the night of the 21st in accordance with 61st Div Art Instructions № 6.

2. Actual hour of departure & route to be followed will be notified later.

3. A Marching Out State in duplicate will be prepared by HQ. & both Sections, one copy of which will be sent to HQ. on the evening of the 21st.

4. Lieut R.G.B Chase is detailed for duty at GODWAERSVELDE in accordance with para. 7.

5. Orders contained in 61 Div Art instructions № 6. paras 6, 8 & 10 – 15 will be closely followed.

6. All Sections are reminded that on leaving the WATOU Artillery Area Wagon parks & horse lines are left scrupulously clean.

7. Sgt Morris (HQ Staff.) will be responsible for obtaining a certificate from the Camp Warden that the area occupied by this unit has been left in a satisfactory condition.

8. The T.M. personnel detailed under para 17 will be distributed between SAA Sect. & 'B' Echelon.

9. Orders in regard to disposal of area stores & supply arrangements will be issued later.

10. ACKNOWLEDGE.

Copy № 1 – RSM
" " 2 – O.B. SAA SECT.
" " 3 – O.B. 'B' ECH.
" " 4 – WAR DIARY

T. Alston
Captain
Commdg 61 D.A.C.

War Diary

Appendix A

March Orders

for S.A.A. Section "B" Echelon D.A.C.

By Captain J R Alston

Commanding 61st Divisional Ammn Column.

Reference Map: Belgium & France Sht 27 NE
Lens Sht: 11.

1. The S.A.A. Section & B Echelon will move from the WATOU Artillery Area to GODWAERSVELDE (entraining station) tomorrow 23rd inst. in accordance with 61 Div. Art. Order No 87 already in possession of Units.

2. The route to be taken for all 3 parties will be as follows:- DROGLANDT STEENVOORDE, H35.d.4.5.

3. The 3 parties will be composed as follows:-

A PARTY.	½ S.A.A. Section	Lieut. H.K. HANSON
B. PARTY.	"B" Echelon.	Lieut: A.S. ALLEN.
C PARTY.	½ S.A.A. Section	Lieut: R.G.B. CHASE.

4. Corpl Mucklow RAMC will accompany "C" party, together with the Medical Cart.

5. Starting Point for each party will be DROGLANDT. Map reference J.12.b.8.6.

6. Time of departure from Starting Point.

A PARTY.	1-0 A.M.
B. PARTY.	5-0. A.M.
C PARTY.	9-15. A.M.

7. Arrangements will be made for guides to meet the train on arrival at ARRAS. to guide Sections to new Wagon Lines.

8. Watches will be synchronised at Headquarters at 5-0 p.m. this afternoon.

9. Sections are again reminded that Wagon, Parks & Horse Lines will be left scrupulously clean.

10. ACKNOWLEDGE.

J R Alston
Captain
Commanding 61 D.A.C.

Appendix A.

March Orders
for
H.Q. 61st D.A.C.
by
Captain T. R. Alston
Comdg. 61st Div. Amm. Col.

Copy No 4

1. H.Q. 61st D.A.C. will move from the WATOU Artillery Area to GODWAERSVELDE (entraining station), tonight 22nd instant

2. The head of the Column will be at DROGLANDT corner ready to move at 9.30 pm

3. The route to be taken will be as follows:- DROGLANDT, STEENVOORDE, H.35 d. 4 5

4. Corpl. Mucklow. RAMC will travel with the S.A.A Section by the train leaving at 3.5 pm tomorrow afternoon and will take orders from Lt R.G.B. Chase.

5. Watches will be synchronised at HQ at 5 pm this afternoon.

6. HQ camp will be left scrupulously clean.

ACKNOWLEDGE

T.R. Alston
Capt. & Adjt
Cdg 61st D.A.C.

Copy No 1 to Adjutant
" " 2 " O/C No 1 Coy. A.S.C.
" " 3 " R.S.M.
" " 4 " WAR DIARY

Appendix B.

Officers Commanding Sections B.9

1. Advanced billeting party as below under the command of Lieut A.J. Pyle. will leave No 1 Section at 4.0. am on the morning of the 21st

2 'B' Echelon will detail a wagon to convey the party to POPERINGHE

3. On arrival at POPERINGHE at 5.15. am the Officer in charge will report to R.T.O. for further instructions

4. Train arrangements for party in accordance with 61st Div. Art. Instructions No 6, schedule B.

5. Rations for 2 days will be carried.

6. Composition of billeting party as follows

Headquarters.	Bdr Gliddon.
No 1 Section.	Cpl Mowbray. a/Bdr Savery.
No 2 Section.	Sgt Cooksey. Bdr Harwood.
SAA Section.	BQMS. Langford. a/Bdr Iles.
'B'. Echelon.	Farr. Sgt Dyke. Bdr Glover.

7. ACKNOWLEDGE.

[signature]
Captain
Commanding 61st D.A.C.

H.Q 61st D.A.C.
20.9.17

Appendix C

COPY No. . 4. . .

March Orders
for No 1 Section D.A.C.
by
Capt T. R. Alston
Commanding 61st Divisional Ammn Column.

---

1. No 1 Section will move from present area in accordance with 61 Div. Art Instructions No 6 attached.

2. O.C. No Section will detach 1 G.S. wagon & 4 ammunition wagons to report with necessary personnel to each battery of the 306 Brigade R.F.A. on the afternoon of the 21st as set out in schedule A of 61. Div. Art Instructions No 6.

3. G.S. wagons will be drawn ready loaded from SAA Section to complete up to required number by arrangements between O.C. Sections

4. O.C. No. 1. Section will at once get into communication with the Adjutant 306. Bde R.F.A. in order to co-ordinate march arrangements for Bde HQ. 306 Bde R.F.A. & the remainder of No 1 Sect's personnel & wagons

5. A complete Marching Out State in accordance with 61 Div. Art Instructions No 6, para 9. will be prepared in duplicate, one copy being forwarded to this office on the evening of Sept 21st, the second copy being retained by O.C. No Section.

6. Orders contained in 61 Div Art Instructions No 6, paras 10--15. will be closely followed.

7. Sections are reminded that before leaving this area, both horselines & wagon parks will be left scrupulously clean.

8. Orders in regard to area stores & supply arrangements will be issued later.

9. ACKNOWLEDGE.

Copy No 1 O.C. No 1 Section
" 2 " SAA "
" 3 Bde RFA.
" 4 War Diary.

T R Alston
Captain
Commanding 61st D.A.C.

Appendix C

COPY No. 4....

March Orders
for No 2 Section D.A.C.
by
Capt T. R. Alston
Commanding 61st Divisional Ammn Column.

1. No 2 Section will move from present area in accordance with 61 Div. Art Instructions No 6 attached.

2. O.C. No 2 Section will detach 1 G.S. wagon & 4 ammunition wagons to report with necessary personnel to each battery of the 307 Brigade R.F.A. on the afternoon of the 21st as set out in schedule A of 61 Div. Art. Instructions No 6.

3. G.S wagons will be drawn ready loaded from SAA Section to complete up to required number by arrangements between O.C Sections

4. O.C. No 2 Section will at once get into communication with the Adjutant 307 Bde R.F.A. in order to co-ordinate march arrangements for Bde H.Q. 307 Bde R.F.A. & the remainder of No 2 Sects personnel & wagons.

5. A complete Marching Out State in accordance with 61 Div. Art. Instructions No 6, para 9. will be prepared in duplicate, one copy being forwarded to this office on the evening of Sept 21st, the second copy being retained by O.C. No 2 Section.

6. Orders contained in 61 Div Art Instructions No 6, paras 10–15. will be closely followed.

7. Sections are reminded that before leaving this area, both horselines & wagon parks will be left scrupulously clean.

8. Orders in regard to area stores & supply arrangements will be issued later.

9. ACKNOWLEDGE.

Copy No 1 O.C No 2 Section.
" " 2 " SAA "
" " 3 Bde RFA.
" " 4 War Diary.

T R Alston
Captain
Commanding 61st D.A.C.

Vol 18

61st Divisional Ammunition Column.

War Diary

From 1st to 31st October 1917.

Vol. 18

Instructions regarding War Diaries and Intelligence Summaries are contained in F. S. Regs., Part II. and the Staff Manual respectively. Title pages will be prepared in manuscript.

WAR DIARY
or
INTELLIGENCE SUMMARY.
(Erase heading not required.)

Army Form C. 2118.

Place	Date	Hour	Summary of Events and Information	Remarks and references to Appendices
Ref Map 51B				
G.13.b	Oct 1st/17		Reorganisation of D.A.C. in accordance with War Estb Part 7A Result of reorganisation (War Estb Part 7A) evacuated personel 43 men + 53 animals.	
L.6.a.2.5	Oct 3rd/17		61st D.A.C. moved from (G.13.b Map 51B). H.Q and A. Echelon to L.6.a.2.5. 3rd Sect to G.11.c. Act. Capt E. Yates to be act Adj vice Capt J. R. Alston. 2nd Lieut K. Baker transferred from S.A.A. Sect to No3 Sect + attached to H.Q as Orderly Officer. Draft of 1 Officer + 109 men from R.H + R.F.A Base Depot and distributed as follows:- 1 Officer + 17 men to 306 Bde. 21 men to D.A.C (7 per Sect) 11 men to T.M., 60 men to 307 Bde Lieut. A. S. Allen (3rd Sect) and party of 10 men from No1 Sect attd to 306 Bde Lieut G. H. Gibbs (2nd Sect) and party of 10 men from No2 Sect attd to 307 Bde 2nd Lieut Millward and 10 men from 306 Bde, 2nd Lieut Millward to 3rd Sect and 10 men to No1 Sect. 2nd Lieut E.S. Port and 10 men from 307 Bde and attached to No2 Sect.	Appendix A

T2134. Wt. W708–776. 500000. 4/15. Sir J. C. & S.

Instructions regarding War Diaries and Intelligence Summaries are contained in F. S. Regs., Part II. and the Staff Manual respectively. Title pages will be prepared in manuscript.

WAR DIARY
or
INTELLIGENCE SUMMARY.
(Erase heading not required.)

Army Form C. 2118.

Place	Date	Hour	Summary of Events and Information	Remarks and references to Appendices
L.6.a.2.5	Oct 2/17		Inspection of H.Q + A Echelon Horse Lines by the CRA accompanied by the SCRA	
	Oct 4/17		Lieut W.H. Sutcliffe reported for duty and attached No 2 Section	
	Oct 5/17		The DDVS accompanied by the ADVS XVII Corps inspected the horses of this Unit.	
			Lieut C A Thurley reported back from Physical Training Course.	
	Oct 8/17		Lieut C A Thurley left for the XVII Corps Heavy Artillery HQ for six weeks attachment	
			Draft of 29 men from base, viz 1 Sergt, 2 Bdrs, + 26 other ranks	
	Oct 10/17		Draft of 29 men were disposed of as follows:-	
			1 Sergt, 1 Bdr + 10 other ranks to 306 Bde	
			1 Bdr + 14 other ranks to 307th Bde. 2 other ranks to Div Ammn Col	
			Lieut R G B Chase left for Abbeville with 18 G S Wagons + 38 animals surplus to re-organisation, and returned on the 12/10/17, + posted to No 1 Section	
	Oct 11/17		Capt T R Alston proceeded on 1 months leave, Capt E Yates act/Adj in command of the 61st Div Ammn Col during his absence.	
	Oct 12/17		Inspection of H.Q + A Echelon Horse Lines by the CRA accompanied by the SCRA	

Army Form C. 2118.

Instructions regarding War Diaries and Intelligence Summaries are contained in F. S. Regs., Part II. and the Staff Manual respectively. Title pages will be prepared in manuscript.

WAR DIARY
or
INTELLIGENCE SUMMARY.
(Erase heading not required.)

Place	Date	Hour	Summary of Events and Information	Remarks and references to Appendices
	Oct 12/17		Received a visit from the Corps Major for Horse Management	
	Oct 14/17		Commencement of Signalling Course under Lieut Hendrie B/306 Bde 10 men from the D.A.C are attending this course.	
	Oct 10/17		Lieut W.H. Sutcliffe (attached No 2 Sect) + party of 10 men attached to ~~306~~ 307 Bde	
			Party of 10 men from No 1 Sect attached to 306 Bde	
			2nd Lieut A. Bostock and 10 men from 306 Bde attached to No 1 Section	
			Party of 10 men from 307 Bde attached to No 2 Section	
G.13.D.7.4 Sheet 51B	Oct 16/17		All horses of the D.A.C were dipped.	
	Oct 16/17		No 3 Section moved into their new quarters L.6.a.2.5.	
	Oct 15/17		2 Lieut F G Cox posted to the 61st Div Art from 187 Bde R.F.A and posted to No 1 Section for duty.	
	Oct 19/17		The following officers reported from Base as reinforcements and have been posted as follows:- 2 Lieut Bridge C.R to 306 Bde. 2nd Lieut H A Digby to 2nd Lieut S.D. Gillam to 307 Bde 2nd Lieut G.M. Lane to D.A.C and attached to No 3 Section	
	Oct 22/17		Colonel S.D. Browne C.B RA took over command of the 61st D.A.C	

T2134. Wt. W708—776. 500000. 4/15. Sir J. C. & S.

Instructions regarding War Diaries and Intelligence Summaries are contained in F. S. Regs., Part II. and the Staff Manual respectively. Title pages will be prepared in manuscript.

WAR DIARY
or
INTELLIGENCE SUMMARY.
(Erase heading not required.)

Army Form C. 2118.

Place	Date	Hour	Summary of Events and Information	Remarks and references to Appendices
	Oct 26/17		Received a visit from the Corps Major for Horse Management accompanied by the Staff Capt R.A.	
	28/17		Received a visit from the G.O.C. 61st Div + G.O.C. R.A. + made an inspection of the Horse Lines, Stables, Billets etc	
	29/17		Two Officers + twenty men to Bdes for instruction:- 2nd Lieut Lane and 10 men to 307 Bde accompanied by 2nd Lieut Pont. Lieut J. James + 10 men to 306 Bde. accompanied by 2nd Lieut Bostock. Lieut Kilby + 10 men from 307 Bde attached to No 1 Section. Lieut Sutcliffe + 10 men to No 2 Section. Lieut Gibbs returned from a course of instruction from A/307 Bde + posted to No 3 Section	
	30/17.		Lieut Pyle, Lieut Hawson + 4 N.C.Os proceeded to Rouen on a course of instruction at the Indian Cavalry Advance Base Depot	

E. Yates Capt + Adj
for Lieut. Colonel. R.F.A.
Commanding 61st (S.M.) Div. Amm. Col.

T2134. Wt. W708—776. 500000. 4/15. Sir J. C. & S.

Appendix A.

COPY Nº 7

March Orders
for Tuesday October 2nd 1917.
by
Capt T.R. Alston.
Commanding 61st Divisional Ammn Column.

1/ Headquarters, Nos 1, 2 & 3 Sections of 61 D.A.C. will move to new wagon lines tomorrow morning 2nd Oct.

2/ Sections will move under the orders of their own Section Commanders.

3/ Headquarters Office will close at G.13.b. at 10.am tomorrow & open at L.6.a.2.5. at the same hour.

4/ Sections will immediately report to Headquarters on arrival in new wagon lines.

5/ All tents which were drawn on arrival in this area will be struck & dumped in the Details lines & receipts obtained for them from Lt R.G.B. Chase.

6/ The Details of the SAA Section under the command of Lieut R.G.B Chase will remain in their present wagon lines until further orders are received as to disposal.

7/ ACKNOWLEDGE.

T.R. Alston
Captain
Commanding 61 D.A.C.

COPY Nº 1 to OC Nº 1 Sect.
" 2 " OC " 2 "
" 3 " OC " 3 "
" 4 " OFFR i/c Details
" 5 " ADJT.
" 6 " RSM.
" 7 " WAR DIARY.

W. 15517—M. 141. 250,000. 1/16. L. S. & Co. Forms/W 3091/2.

Army Form W. 3091.

Confidential

Cover for Documents.

61st DAC

Nature of Enclosures.

War Diary

Volume 19.

Period 1 - 30 Nov 1917

Notes, or Letters written.

4

4

Instructions regarding War Diaries and Intelligence Summaries are contained in F. S. Regs., Part II. and the Staff Manual respectively. Title pages will be prepared in manuscript.

WAR DIARY
or
INTELLIGENCE SUMMARY.
(Erase heading not required.)

Army Form C. 2118.

61 D Am Col
Vol

Place	Date	Hour	Summary of Events and Information	Remarks and references to Appendices
ANZIN ST AUBIN	Nov 7th	10.30 am	Received a visit from the C.R.A 61st Div Art accompanied by the	
" "			Staff Capt R.A. + Instructor in Catering for 3rd Army. An inspection of Cook houses was made and lectures delivered on Messing.	
" "	Nov 11th		Received a visit from the C.R.A 61st Div accompanied by Staff Capt R.A. inspected H.Qrs and Sections Wagon Lines	
" "	Nov 12th		Capt J. R. Alston resumes the duties of Adjutant on returning from leave	
" "	Nov 12th		Capt E. Yates remains attached to Headquarters as Orderly Officer	
" "	Nov 13th		3 Gunners reported to 'K' A.A. Battery, Haute Avesnes for a course of Flash Spotting	
" "	Nov 13th		Lieut Kilby attached to No 1 Sect D.A.C. returned to 307th Bde also 10 O.R. 10 OR returned to 306 Bde	
" "			Lieut F. G. Lester Officer i/c Bomb Store, Lieut G. Arsell i/c Horse Shoe Dump together with 5 men from No 1 Sect + 5 men from No 2 Sect attached to 307 Bde.	
" "	Nov 15		CAPT P.H. LUDLOW ~~[illegible]~~ i/c No 2 Section evacuated to Hospital	
" "	"		Lieut E. YATES orderly officer, is appointed to the command of No 2 Section with the rank of acting captain vice Capt P.H. LUDLOW as and from to-day's date.	

T2134. Wt. W708—776. 500000. 4/15. Sir J. C. & S.

Instructions regarding War Diaries and Intelligence Summaries are contained in F. S. Regs., Part II. and the Staff Manual respectively. Title pages will be prepared in manuscript.

WAR DIARY
or
INTELLIGENCE SUMMARY.
(Erase heading not required.)

Army Form C. 2118.

Place	Date	Hour	Summary of Events and Information	Remarks and references to Appendices
ANZIN				
ST AUBIN	16:11:17		CAPT A.G.B. SPEAR, CAPT E. YATES & 3 Section cooks visited 3rd Army School of Cookery ALBERT	
"	"	"	Lieut W.H. SUTCLIFFE returned from Physical Drill Course at 3rd Army Artillery Training School	
"	"	17:11:17	Colonel S.D. BROWNE comdg 61 D.A.C. proceeded on leave (14 days) to ENGLAND	
"	"	"	CAPT T.R. ALSTON assumed command of 61 D.A.C	
"	"	"	Lieut J.T. JAMES (No 2 Section) attached for duty to No 1 Section	
"	"	"	4.30 pm	No 1 Section moved from ANZIN area to BEAULENCOURT to work in conjunction with 306 Art Bde march orders (appendix 'A') attached (authority for move IV Corps)	
"	"	18:11:17		No 1 Section reported arrival at BEAULENCOURT at 4 am. 18:11:17	
"	"	17:11:17		2 gunners returned from course at 3rd Army T.M. School	
"	"	16:11:17		Lieut G.H. GIBBS (No 3 Section) proceeded on 14 days leave to England	
"	"	22:11:17		Lieut W.H. SUTCLIFFE relieved Lt R.M. MONTGOMERY at ANZIN No 1 DUMP	
"	"	"		Lieut R.M. MONTGOMERY proceeded to ENGLAND on 14 days leave	
"	"	21:11:17		8 O.R. proceed on a course to 3rd Army T.M. School LIGNY-ST-FLOCHEL	
"	"	23:11:17	12 midday	G.O.C.R.A. with S.C.R.A. inspected Nos 2 & 3 Section horse lines	
"	"	24:11:17		ANZIN DUMP No 1 closed (authority XVII Corps wire A11/920 of 23/11) Lieut W.H. SUTCLIFFE returns to No 2 Section	
"	"	25:11:17	5.20 pm	2nd Lt F.G.L. COX with party of 20 Drivers and 1 Shoeing Smith proceeded by train to ABBEVILLE for collection of 39 Remounts	

T2131. Wt. W708–776. 500000. 4/15. Sir J. C. & S.

Instructions regarding War Diaries and Intelligence Summaries are contained in F. S. Regs., Part II. and the Staff Manual respectively. Title pages will be prepared in manuscript.

WAR DIARY
or
INTELLIGENCE SUMMARY.
(Erase heading not required.)

Army Form C. 2118.

Place	Date	Hour	Summary of Events and Information	Remarks and references to Appendices
ANZIN ST AUBIN	26:11:17	11-30 am	A.D.V.S XVII Corps inspected the animals of the 61 D.A.C (less No 1 Section)	[illegible]
"	25:11:17		A/Cpl ELKINS E.J. (No 1 Section) proceeded to XVII Corps Gas School AGNEZ-les-DUISANS	[illegible]
"	26:11:17		Capt N.C. BENNETT, D.A.A.G 61 DW inspected work on horse standings No 3 Section	[illegible]
"	27:11:17		Lt A.J. PYLE & 2 N.C.O's returned from an Indian Training Course at the Indian Cavalry Advanced Base Depot ROUEN	[illegible]
"	26:11:17		Revised War Establishment No 818 Part VII A received	[illegible]
"	28:11:17	6.20 am	Lt A J PYLE with party of 16 O.R. proceeded by train from ARRAS to YTRES to rejoin No 1 Section D.A.C.	306 Bde [illegible]
"	"		4 O.R. returned from Course of Flash Spotting for Trench Mortars at Depot Field Survey Coy MONTREUIL	[illegible]
"	"		2nd Lt F.G.L. COX & party returned from ABBEVILLE with 39 Remounts (horses) which were distributed as follows	306 26, 307 9, D.A.C 4
"	30:11:17		Temporary R.S.M. WEBSTER reported for duty to 306 Bde RFA	
"	"		26 Remounts for 306 Bde taken down by road and delivered to the Bde by R.S.M. Webster	[illegible]
"	"		Lt J.T. JAMES returned from No 1 Section & was reported for duty to No 2 Section	[illegible]

[illegible] Capt Major
Comdg 61 D.A.C.

T2134. Wt. W708—776. 500000. 4/15. Sir J. C. & S.

Appendix A

3.156/

March Orders
by
Capt. J. R. Alston
Comdg. 61st Div. Amm. Col.
for
17th NOVEM. 1917.

Copy No. 2

Ref. Map. LENS. 11. 1/100.000

1/ No. 1 Section, 61st D.A.C. will move from their present station to BEAULENCOURT, under the orders of the O.C. Section.

2/ The route to be taken will be as follows:- ARRAS, main road to BAPAUME, BEAULENCOURT.

3/ Time of departure. 4-30pm.

4/ On arrival at BAPAUME the Officer Commanding will send forward an officer to report to the Area Commandant 'M' area at BEAULENCOURT.

5/ The completion of the move will be wired to IV Corps HQ and 61st D.A.C.H.Q.

6/ The usual 10 minutes to the hour halts will be taken and a long halt of an hour at the discretion of the Officer Commanding.

7/ The present camp will be left clean and arrangements will be made for stores which are being left behind to be neatly packed.

8/ Signal time will be obtained from HQ. at 3pm this afternoon.

ACKNOWLEDGE

Copy No. 1 to O/C No. 1 Section
" 2 War Diary.
" 3 File.

Captain
Cdg. 61st D.A.C.

61ST DIVISION

61ST DIVL AMMN COLUMN

MAY 1916-MAY 1919

Confidential War Diary V/A 20

61st Div Am Col

Period 1 – 31 December 1917

Volume. 20

Instructions regarding War Diaries and Intelligence Summaries are contained in F. S. Regs., Part II. and the Staff Manual respectively. Title pages will be prepared in manuscript.

WAR DIARY
or
INTELLIGENCE SUMMARY.
(Erase heading not required.)

Army Form C. 2118.

Place	Date	Hour	Summary of Events and Information	Remarks and references to Appendices
	1:12:17		Headquarters } No. 2 Section } ANZIN St AUBIN near ARRAS; No. 3 Section } No 1 Section HAVRINCOURT Wood between METZ and TRESCAULT	
ANZIN St AUBIN	"		Lt J.T. JAMES (No 2 Section) reported to O/C "K" A.A. Battery (attached 306 Art Bde) (HAUTE-AVESNES) for month's Course	
"	"		2nd Lt P.A.V. PEACOCKE (C/306) reported for duty & was attached to No 3 Section	
"	"		a/c Bomb. ELKINS E.J. returned from a Course at the Corps gas School AGNEZ-les-DUISSANS	
"	2.12.17		B.S.M. THORNTON D/306 reported for duty as R.S.M.	
"	3.12.17	1.40 pm	S.A.A. Section moved from present station to BAPAUME under orders of Capt H. B. DONE (authority telegram G.B. 834 XVII Corps)	March orders (appendix A)
"	"		Colonel S.A. BROWNE C.B. R.G. assumed Command of 61 D.A.C. on returning from leave, vice Capt T.R. ALSTON	
"	4:12:17		S.A.A. Section moved from BAPAUME to EQUANCOURT	
"	"		Capt H.B DONE (O.C. SAA Section) admitted to Hospital, Lieut A.S. ALLEN assumes command of S.A.A. Section	
"	5:12:17		Lieut G H GIBBS returned from leave & proceeded at once to BAPAUME to rejoin his Section	
"	"		Lieut A.S. ALLEN & 2nd Lt P.A.V. PEACOCKE both wounded and admitted to Hospital } Hostile shelling EQUANCOURT	
"	"		2 O.R killed and 4 wounded (all S.A.A Section).	
"	6:12:17	a/c	Capt E. YATES appointed to command (temporary) of S.A.A Section, & proceeded to EQUANCOURT	
"	"		2nd Lt F.G.L. COX appointed to command of No 2 Section during absence of Capt E. YATES	
"	22:11:17		CAPT P.H. LUDLOW evacuated to ENGLAND, sick, & struck off the strength of the 61 D.A.C. with effect from that date	
"	5:12:17		2nd Lt K. BAKER returned from duty at HORSESHOE DUMP & proceeded to EQUANCOURT to rejoin No 3 Section	

T2134. Wt. W708—776. 500000. 4/15. Sir J. C. & S.

Instructions regarding War Diaries and Intelligence Summaries are contained in F. S. Regs., Part II. and the Staff Manual respectively. Title pages will be prepared in manuscript.

WAR DIARY
or
INTELLIGENCE SUMMARY.
(Erase heading not required.)

Army Form C. 2118.

Place	Date	Hour	Summary of Events and Information	Remarks and references to Appendices
ANZIN ST AUBIN	8.12.17		Lieut R.M. MONTGOMERY (No 2 Section) returned from Leave	
"	9.12.17		Lieut R.M. MONTGOMERY reported at HQ Royal Flying Corps (via HESDIN) for duty as an observer for the R.F.C. & is struck off strength from date of joining	
"	"		Following postings of officers to take effect from the 9th inst Lieut G.H. GIBBS No 3 Section DAC to A/307 2/Lt H. BUCKETT from A/307 to No 3 Section DAC 2 Lieut F.J.E. PRATT No 1 Section DAC to D/306	
"	19.12.17	9am	Headquarters 61 D.A.C. moved from ANZIN to EQUANCOURT Route as follows – ARRAS BOIRY – BECQUERELLE, BOYELLES, ERVILLERS, BÉHAGNIES, SAPIGNIES, BAPAUME, BEAULENCOURT, le TRANSLOY, ROCQUIGNY, le MESNIL-en-ARROUAISE, MANANCOURT, ETRICOURT, EQUANCOURT (time of arrival 7.10pm)	
EQUANCOURT	20.12.17		Map References of HQ & Sections in EQUANCOURT AREA: Headquarters V.10.d central; No 1 Section V.3.d.4.2.; S.A.A Section V.10.d.9.6. Reference map 57C	
"	26.12.17	10.30 am	Headquarters No 1 & SAA Section moved from EQUANCOURT AREA to BEAULENCOURT, Route as follows – ETRICOURT, LECHELLE, BUS, ROCQUIGNY, LE TRANSLOY. Headquarters office opened on night of 28/12/17 at BUIRE SUR L'ANCRE	
"	27.12.17		March continued by Headquarters No 1 & S.A.A Section to LE BARQUE on ALBERT–BAPAUME Rd via BAPAUME	
"	28.12.17		" by road to BUIRE sur L'ANCRE Route as follows le SARS, POZIÈRES, ALBERT, DERNANCOURT	
"	"		The following officers reported for duty & were posted as follows: 2/Lt C.A. KEOGH No 1 Section; 2/Lt H.A. BLUNDELL No 2 Section; 2/Lt D. ROGERS SAA Section	

T2131. Wt. W708–776. 500000. 4/15. Sir J. C. & S.

Instructions regarding War Diaries and Intelligence Summaries are contained in F. S. Regs., Part II. and the Staff Manual respectively. Title pages will be prepared in manuscript.

WAR DIARY
or
INTELLIGENCE SUMMARY.
(Erase heading not required.)

Army Form C. 2118.

Place	Date	Hour	Summary of Events and Information	Remarks and references to Appendices
	25.12.17	6.30 am	No 2 Section 61 DAC left ANZIN for BAPAUME (under orders from 15 Division) Route main ARRAS-BAPAUME Road	[initials]
	26.12.17	9 am	" " " - BAPAUME for BUIRE sur L'ANCRE, but only reached LE BARQUE owing to condition of roads. Subsequently proceeding under orders of C.O. 61 DAC with the remainder of the Column	[initials]
	29.12.17		61 D.A.C rested at BUIRE sur L'ANCRE	
	30.12.17	9.20 am	61 D.A.C moved from BUIRE sur L'ANCRE to SAILLY-LAURETTE via VILLE-sous-CORBIE & MORLANCOURT	Appendix C
	31.12.17	11 am	61 D.A.C moved from SAILLY-LAURETTE to CAYEUX-en-Santerre, Route WARFUSEE-ABANCOURT - MARCELCAVE, AUBERCOURT, IGNAUCOURT	Appendix D.
CAYEUX	" "		The undermentioned officers were posted to Brigades as follows & reported for duty: Lieut W.H. SUTCLIFFE, 2/Lt D. ROGERS, 2/Lt H.A. BLUNDELL to 307 Bde, 2/Lt C.A. KEOGH to 306 Bde	[initials]

[signature] Capt [illegible]
for Col Comdg 61 D.A.C

Copy No 2

SECRET

Appendix A

3 of 3

Move Orders
by
Captain J R Alston
for
S A A Section 6th Divl Ammn Column

Reference Map LENS Sheet 11

1 The S A A Section will move from present area to BAPAUME under the orders of Captain H B Dene
2 Time of starting 1-0 PM
3 Route to be taken ARRAS - BAPAUME ROAD
4 Echelon will march full of ammunition
5 The following wagons will report to S A A Section at 8 0 AM 3/12/17

1 G S from T M Battery
1 " " " No 2 Section

6 Baggage & Supply wagons will report at 9-0 am
7 Rations & Forage for 4th inst will be issued.
8 Billets from Town Major BAPAUME for night 3-4th will be arranged by S C R A
9 Usual 10 minutes to the hour halt will be taken
10 Watches will be synchronized at HQ Signal Office at 11.0 AM 3/4/17
11 Further orders for move on the 4th inst will be issued later
12 ACKNOWLEDGE

Copy No 1 OC No 3 Section
2 " 2 "
3 War Diary
4 File

J R Alston
Captain Adjutant
Commanding 6 D A C

2 12 1917

Copy No

Appendix B

[illegible]

25th [illegible]

[illegible]

[illegible]

[illegible]

1\. The 6th R.H.A., [illegible] No 2 Section, will [illegible] from the present area to the TREUX area [illegible] of [illegible] on the [illegible] road.

2\. Starting point [illegible] BRIDGE [illegible] 10.30 [illegible]

3\. The route to be taken will be as follows: [illegible], BUS, [illegible], [illegible].

4\. H.Q. will form the [illegible] and will move so as to be at the starting point at 10.30 a.m. [illegible] will be [illegible] to move with the [illegible] of the Column at the [illegible] at the same time. [illegible] Section will not go on to the main [illegible] road until No [illegible] Section are clear of the [illegible] corner.

5\. Baggage wagons will report to the wagon lines at [illegible] a.m. [illegible]

6\. A lorry will be [illegible] for [illegible] at [illegible] will [illegible] the lorry and report to Capt [illegible] at [illegible]

7\. Lt [illegible] will act as Billeting Officer and will report at [illegible] at [illegible] to proceed by lorry to the [illegible] at TREUX.

8\. [illegible] will proceed in charge of the mounted billeting party, consisting of [illegible] of each Section [illegible]. The [illegible] from [illegible] Section will [illegible]. The party will form [illegible] at [illegible] a.m. and will report to the Staff Captain R.A. at TREUX [illegible] at [illegible].

9\. A distance of 100 yards will be maintained between H.Q. and Sections.

10\. Each Section will detail a mounted N.C.O. to report to [illegible] at [illegible] for [illegible] of watches.

11\. The usual 10 minute [illegible] halts will be taken [illegible] from the head of the column.

12\. Supply wagons will [illegible] at TREUX [illegible] H.Q. and Sections will [illegible] at TREUX [illegible].

13\. Advance billeting party will arrange [illegible] billets; [illegible]

ACKNOWLEDGE

Copy No 1 - [illegible] Officer
2 - O/C No 1 Section
3 - [illegible] 2 [illegible]
4 - R.S.M.
5 - [illegible] Diary
6 - File

[illegible]

5

(Appendix C)

1. [illegible]

EAA No 2

2. [illegible]

3. [illegible]

4. [illegible]

5. [illegible]

6. [illegible]

7. [illegible]

8. [illegible]

9. [illegible]

10. [illegible]

11. [illegible]

12. [illegible]

13. [illegible]

14.

ACKNOWLEDGE.

Copy No 1 [illegible]
2
3
4 R.E. [illegible]
5 [illegible]

Copy No.

Appendix D

March Orders
for
31st 12-17
by
Col. S. & D. Browne C.B.
Cdg. 61st Div. Amm. Col.

Ref. Map. AMIENS. 17

1. The 61st D.A.C. will move from SAILLY LAURETTE to CAYEUX-EN-SANTERRE

2. Starting point Cross Roads 1000 yards South of the church in SAILLY LAURETTE. Time 11 am

3. Order of march, H.Q., No 1 Section, SAA Section, R.A. HQ, No 2 Section.

4. Route to be taken is as follows:- WARFUSEE, MARCELCAVE, outskirts of DEMUIN, AUBERCOURT, IGNAUCOURT.

5. Lt. R. G. B. Chase will leave the Church SAILLY LAURETTE in charge of the billeting party, constituted as before, at 8-30 am

6. 2/Lt. K. Baker will inspect billets so after the Unit has marched out, and will obtain a certificate from the Town Major that he is satisfied with the condition of billets, wagon parks and horse lines. The certificate obtained will be handed in to this office on arrival in the new area.

7. Orders for today in regard to the maintaining of distances between units and subsections will be continued.

8. ACKNOWLEDGE

Copy No. 1 No 1 Section
" " 2 " 2 "
" " 3 S.A.A. "
" " 4 R.S.M.
" " 5 War Diary.

R. Aston
Capt & Adjt
for Colonel
Cdg 61 D.A.C.

Lieut R. G. B. Chase will report to the adjutant at Headquarters Mess before departure in the morning

Instructions regarding War Diaries and Intelligence Summaries are contained in F. S. Regs., Part II. and the Staff Manual respectively. Title pages will be prepared in manuscript.

WAR DIARY
or
INTELLIGENCE SUMMARY.
(Erase heading not required.)

Army Form C. 2118.

61 D Am Col

Vol 21

Place	Date	Hour	Summary of Events and Information	Remarks and references to Appendices
CAYEUX-EN-SANTERRE	1.1.18		CAPT E YATES re assumed command of No 2 Section vice 2/Lt F G L COX	
"	"		Lieut R G S CHASE (No 1 Section) is transferred to S.A.A. Section and to take over command of the Section [illegible]	
			Capt E YATES during the absence of CAPT H E DONE, admitted to hospital sick	
"	2.1.18		The following transfers of officers to take effect from to-day's date	
			Lieut G M GIBBS from S A A Section to No 2 Section	
			2/Lt H G ANSELL " No 2 " S.A.A "	
			2/Lt K BAKER " S A A " No 1 "	
"	" 1.1.18		2/Lt G R SOWTER reported for duty from the Base, & was posted to No 2 Section	
	2.1.18		The following officers reported from the Base for duty & were posted as follows –	
			2/Lieut S J HYDE (No 1 Section) 2/Lt G M McCAIG (S.A.A Section)	
			45 Remounts (51 L D Horses) collected from LA CHAPELETTE by 2/Lt H G ANSELL & collecting party & were distributed as follows No 1 Section 11 No 2 Section 6 No 3 Section 28	
"	" 6.1.18		Lieut A J PYLE proceeded in charge of a party of 57 O R to collect Remounts from CHAUNES & distributed as follows.	51 L.D. Horses as to drawn
"	" 9.1.18	11 am	61 D A C marched from CAYEUX to ROYE AREA route CAIX LE QUESNEL, BOUCHOIR, ROYE (March orders Appendix A attached)	
ROYE	10.1.18	9.15 am	No 2 Section 61 D A C moved from ROYE to QUIVIÈRES route RÉTHONVILLERS LANGUEVOISIN, VOYENNES & MATIGNY	Appx B
	11.1.18	9.40	61 D A C (less No 2 Section) moved from ROYE to VILLERS ST CHRISTOPHE route CARRÉPUIS, RÉTHONVILLERS NESLE VOYENNES, BUNY, MATIGNY, TOULLE & SANCOURT (March orders Appendix C)	

T2134. Wt. W708—776. 500000. 4/15. Sir J. C. & S.

Instructions regarding War Diaries and Intelligence Summaries are contained in F. S. Regs., Part II. and the Staff Manual respectively. Title pages will be prepared in manuscript.

WAR DIARY
or
INTELLIGENCE SUMMARY.

(Erase heading not required.)

Army Form C. 2118.

Place	Date	Hour	Summary of Events and Information	Remarks and references to Appendices
VILLERS St CHRISTOPHE	13.1.18		No 2 Section 61 DAC moved from QUIVIÈRES to VILLERS St CHRISTOPHE	g
"	15.1.18		315 BAC moved from UGNY L'EQUIPEE to VILLERS St CHRISTOPHE, and came under the orders of CO. 61 D.A.C on arrival in the VILLERS St CHRISTOPHE AREA	g
"	"		2Lt K BAKER (No 1 Section) transferred from 61 D Arty to 9 D. Arty, is struck off strength from today's date	g
"	"		2Lt S. J. HYDE (No 1 Section) is appointed Town Major of VILLERS St CHRISTOPHE	
"	7.1.18		Lieut A S ALLEN & 2Lt W. F BOOTH reported for duty	
"	8.1.18		2Lt W F BOOTH proceeded to report to 307 A.F.A Bde (in accordance with RAQ 200/45)	
"	"		The following transfers will take effect as from today's date – Lt A S ALLEN from BASE is posted to SAA Section; 2Lt K HAWSON from No 2 Section to SAA Section, 2Lt G M McCAIG from S.A.A Section to No 2 Section	
"	9.1.18		CAPT T R ALSTON proceeded to RAHQ for attachment as Staff Captain vice Capt F W N CRIPPS to ENGLAND	
			LIEUT R.G.B. CHASE was appointed acting Adjutant vice CAPT T R. ALSTON	
"	20.1.18		LIEUT. C.A THURLEY posted to 48th Siege Battery with effect from 10.1.18.	
"	"		2/LIEUT C R BOWYER & 6 OTHER RANKS proceeded on 5th Army T.M. Course	
"	"		Draft of 43 O.R. reported from BASE DEPOT & were posted to Units of 61st Div. Arty as follows. — 306th Bgde RFA 13 O.R.: 307th Bgde 20 O.R. DAC 10 O.R.	
"	23.1.18		CAPT. H. B. DONE reported for duty	

T2134. Wt. W708–776. 500000. 4/15. Sir J. C. & S.

Instructions regarding War Diaries and Intelligence Summaries are contained in F. S. Regs., Part II. and the Staff Manual respectively. Title pages will be prepared in manuscript.

WAR DIARY
or
INTELLIGENCE SUMMARY.
(Erase heading not required.)

Army Form C. 2118.

Place	Date	Hour	Summary of Events and Information	Remarks and references to Appendices
VILLERS ST CHRISTOPHE	23.1.18		2nd LIEUT G.M. McCAIG was attached to 61st Div "A"	[illegible]
" "	25.1.18		" " " reported for duty	[illegible]
" "	27.1.18		2nd LIEUT G.K. STANLEY reported for duty from England & posted No 1 SECTION	[illegible]
" "	29.1.18		CAPT H.B. DONE evacuated to Artillery Base Depot, Harfleur (authority DGMS 445/1 dated 19.1.17)	[illegible]
" "			2/LIEUT R.A.R. ALLEN reported for duty from England, posted to No 1 SECTION	[illegible]
" "			DRAFT 25 O.R. reported from Base Depot & posted as follows 306 Bgde 24 O.R. DAC 1 O.R.	[illegible]
" "			LIEUT A.S. ALLEN proceeded to the 5th ARMY School of Sanitation to attend a course	[illegible]
" "	31.1.18		DRAFT 2 NCO's + 23 O.R. reported from Base	[illegible]

Robert C.B. Chase
Lieut + Adjt
61 DAC

T2134. Wt. W708—776. 500000. 4/15. Sir J. C. & S.

61st Divl Ammunition Column Vol 22

War Diary

1st Feb. 1918 to 28th Feb. 1918.

Vol: 22

Instructions regarding War Diaries and Intelligence Summaries are contained in F. S. Regs., Part II. and the Staff Manual respectively. Title pages will be prepared in manuscript.

WAR DIARY
or
INTELLIGENCE SUMMARY.
(Erase heading not required.)

Army Form C. 2118.

Place	Date	Hour	Summary of Events and Information	Remarks and references to Appendices
VILLERS STE [illegible]	1/7/18			
HQ [illegible]	[illegible]/18		LIEUT CHASE returned to #3 as section Commander	Ra
	[illegible]		Lieut RAP ALLEN appointed acting Adjutant	Ra
	[illegible]		Draft of 2 NCO & 23 O.R. posted to 306 Bde.	Ra
	[illegible]		2nd LT R S CLARKE reported for duty & posted to #1 section	Ra
	[illegible]		2nd LT C R BOWYER returned from 5th Army T.M. [illegible]	Ra
	[illegible]		2nd LT AHG BANNISTER reported for duty & posted to #3 section	Ra
	[illegible]		Draft of 1 NCO & 1 O.R. reported from Base &	Ra.
			posted as follows, NCO to 307 Bde. O.R. to DAC	Ra
	[illegible]		Capt. DONE granted 3 weeks special leave to U.K.	Ra
	[illegible]		3 L D Horses & 15 L D Mules rec'd from 3 [illegible] Depot	Ra
	[illegible]		1 Riding Horse rec'd from 307 Bde	Ra
	[illegible]		Draft of 41 O.R. arrived from Base & posted as	Ra
			follows – [illegible] O.R. DAC, 1 O.R. – DTMO, 22 O.R. – 306 Bde	Ra
			17 – O.R. 307 Bde	Ra
	5/7/18		2nd Lt ROBINSON reported from Base & posted to SAA [illegible]	Ra
	11/7/18		Lt S M McCAIG proceeded on course of [illegible]	Ra
			[illegible] to 5th Army [illegible] School	Ra

T2131. Wt. W708–776. 500000. 4/15. Sir J. C. & S.

Instructions regarding War Diaries and Intelligence Summaries are contained in F. S. Regs., Part II. and the Staff Manual respectively. Title pages will be prepared in manuscript.

WAR DIARY
or
INTELLIGENCE SUMMARY.
(Erase heading not required.)

Army Form C. 2118.

Place	Date	Hour	Summary of Events and Information	Remarks and references to Appendices
[illegible] Ste	19/5/18			
Christophe			1 R. & File recd from 2/5 Warwicks	RA
Quiveres	20/5/18		61. DAC moved from V Ste Christophe to	RA
"	"		Quiveres. (appendix A attached)	RA
"	"		315 BAC move from V. Ste Christophe to	RA
"			Douvieux under O.C. DAC	RA
"	26		315 B.A.C. moved from Douvieux to Buny	RA
"			under orders of O.C. 315 Bde AFA.	RA
"			11 L.D. 97 mules recd from Remount Depot	RA
"	27		2/Lt AHG Bannister proceeded on Anti Gas	RA
			course at XVIII Corps Gas School.	RA

R. A. Rallen
2nd Lt [illegible]
61 - DAC

T2131. Wt. W708—776. 500000. 4/15. Sir J. C. & S.

Instructions regarding War Diaries and Intelligence Summaries are contained in F. S. Regs., Part II. and the Staff Manual respectively. Title pages will be prepared in manuscript.

WAR DIARY
or
INTELLIGENCE SUMMARY.
(Erase heading not required.)

Army Form C. 2118.

6 D Am Col

Vol 23

Place	Date	Hour	Summary of Events and Information	Remarks and references to Appendices
Quevers	1/3/18		Following INDIAN PERSONNEL reported from Base Depot and taken on strength 1 Havildar Major, 2 Havildars 2 Naiks 8 L. Naiks, 36 Gunners 77 Drivers, 3 Langris, 3 Sweepers. LT. HAWSON in charge of the party.	
	5/3/18		Colonel S.D.BROWNE proceeded on 14 days leave to England Captain E. YATES assumed command of D.A.C during the absence of Colonel BROWNE.	
	5/3/18		Lieut J.T. JAMES attached to 5 Army A.A. Group is struck off the strength of the unit.	
	8/3/18		Capt. T.R. ALSTON is attached to R.A H.Q. as Temporary Staff Captain.	
	14/3/18		Following remounts collected & distributed to Bdes 306 Bde = 1 Ride, 1 L.D. 307 Bde 1 Charger, 2 L.D.	

T2131. Wt. W708–776. 500000. 4/15. Sir J. C. & S.

Instructions regarding War Diaries and Intelligence Summaries are contained in F. S. Regs., Part II. and the Staff Manual respectively. Title pages will be prepared in manuscript.

WAR DIARY
or
INTELLIGENCE SUMMARY.
(Erase heading not required.)

Army Form C. 2118.

Place	Date	Hour	Summary of Events and Information	Remarks and references to Appendices
QUIVIERES Ref maps ST QUENTIN Sheet 18 AMIENS Sheet 17	22.3.18	1.45 pm	61 D.A.C moved from QUIVIERES to BUNY via MATIGNY (under verbal orders of G.O.C.R.A 61 Div)	
"	"	9 pm	" " " " BUNY to ETALON Route ROUY-le-GRAND MESNIL-ST-NICAISE MESNIL-le-PETIT MANICOURT & CURCHY	
ETALON	23.3.18		Ammunition Dump formed at H. 8. d 6.3 (Ref Sheet 66D)	
"	24.3.18	10.30 am	61 D.A.C (less SAA Section) moved from ETALON to LIANCOURT FOSSE	
"	"		CAPT T.R. ALSTON returned to D.A.C for duty on completion of attachment to R.A.H.Q.	
"	"	4 pm	61 D.A.C (less SAA Sect) moved from LIANCOURT to FRESNOY-les-ROYE (orders 20 D.A)	
"	"		SAA Section moved from ETALON to HATTENCOURT (orders 61 Div Q)	
FRESNOY	25.3.18		Ammunition Dump formed at G. 29 c 9.0.	
"	"	1.30 pm	61 D.A.C (less SAA Sect) moved from FRESNOY to ANDECHY Route DAMERY la CAMBUSE (orders 20 D.A)	
ANDECHY	"	5 pm	" " " " ANDECHY to BOUCHOIR, SAA Section from HATTENCOURT to GOYENCOURT	
"			Ammunition Dump formed at LA CAMBUSE	
"			" " " BOUCHOIR	
BOUCHOIR	26.3.18	5 am	61 D.A.C (less SAA Sect) moved from BOUCHOIR to LABOISSIERE Route GUERBIGNY LIGNIÈRES (orders 20 D.A)	
LABOISSIERE	"	9 am	" " " " LABOISSIERE to COURTEMANCHE Route FAVEROLLES MONTDIDIER	
COURTEMANCHE	27.3.18	11 am	" " " " COURTEMANCHE to MORISEL Route FRAMICOURT MARESTMONTIERS BOUILLANCOURT HARGICOURT AUBVILLERS, SAUVILLERS-MONGIVAL	orders 20 D.A

T2134. Wt. W708—776. 500000. 4/15. Sir J. C. & S.

Instructions regarding War Diaries and Intelligence Summaries are contained in F. S. Regs., Part II. and the Staff Manual respectively. Title pages will be prepared in manuscript.

WAR DIARY
or
INTELLIGENCE SUMMARY.
(Erase heading not required.)

Army Form C. 2118.

Place	Date	Hour	Summary of Events and Information	Remarks and references to Appendices
	27:3:18		61 D.A.C (less SAA Section) – MORISEL SAA Section – CASTEL intermediate halts for {PARVILLERS LE QUESNEL, GOYENCOURT, MEZIÈRES}	(authority 61 Div Q)
MORISEL	28:3:18	3pm	61 D.A.C (less SAA) moved from MORISEL to JUMEL (Route MON IDÉE – AILLY-sur-NOYE)	(orders 30 D.A)
CASTEL	"		SAA Section moved from CASTEL to GENTELLES (authority 61 Div Q)	
	27:3:18		Ammunition Dump formed at MON IDÉE	
	30:3:18	3pm	61 D.A.C (less SAA) moved from JUMEL to St SAUFLIEU via ORESMAUX (orders 30 D.A)	
	29/3/18–31/3/18		SAA Section moved from GENTELLES to FOUENCAMPS, & subsequently to BOYES–CAGNY Road	(authority 61 Div Q)
	30:3:18		following reinforcements detached to C/307 Bty 10 gunners 10 Drivers & 30 Horses	
	21:3:18		Balance of T.M. personnel officers & men remaining after the fighting of the 21st attached to 61 D.A.C	
	7:3:18		Lieut A.S. ALLEN (SAA Section) struck off strength (Medical Board)	

[illegible] Capt RA
for Col commdg 61 D.A.C

T2134. Wt. W708–776. 500000. 4/15. Sir J. C. & S.

61st Divisional Artillery.

61st DIVISIONAL AMMUNITION COLUMN R.F.A.

APRIL 1918.

Instructions regarding War Diaries and Intelligence Summaries are contained in F. S. Regs., Part II. and the Staff Manual respectively. Title pages will be prepared in manuscript.

WAR DIARY
or
INTELLIGENCE SUMMARY.
(Erase heading not required.)

Army Form C. 2118.

Place	Date	Hour	Summary of Events and Information	Remarks and references to Appendices
Ref. sheet AMIENS 17				
—	1:4:18		HQ, attached Div. personnel, A Echelon & Trench Mortars — St SAUFLIEU	
"			SAA Section D.B.S. & Dump personnel — BOVES-CAGNY Road	
"	2:4:18		2/Lt A. ROBINSON & 2/Lt A.H.G. BANNISTER reported for duty with 306 Bde	
"			Lt R.G.B. CHASE to be actg Capt whilst commdg SAA Section 11:2:18	
"			Lt (actg Capt) H.B. DOWB on ceasing to command SAA Section 11:2:18	
"	6:4:18	5pm	61 D.A.C (less SAA Section) moved from St SAUFLIEU to POIX (orders 20 DA)	
			Route NAMPTY, NEUVILLE-SOUS-LOEUILLY, TAISNIL, NAMPS-au-MONT, QUEVAUVILLERS, FOSSEBLEUET POIX	
Ref. sheet DIEPPE 16	7:4:18	10am	61 DAC (less SAA Section) moved from POIX to BEAUCAMPS le VIEUX (orders area Commandant POIX)	
			Route - EPLESSIER, CAULIÈRES, LIGNIÈRES CHATELAN, MORVILLERS, CHARNY, MONTMARQUET	
"	8:4:18		2/Lt A. ROBINSON & 2/Lt A.H.G BANNISTER reported on completion of temporary attachment to 306 Bde, & were posted for duty as follows. - 2/Lt BANNISTER to No. 1 Section 2/Lt ROBINSON to No. 2 Section	
"	9:4:18		2/Lt CLARK & party returned from Remount Depot ABBEVILLE with 44 LD Horses & 56 mules for the Div. Arty, which were distributed as follows. - 306 Bde 40 Horses {No. 1 Section 27 mules & 3 Horses; No. 2 Section 30 mules}	
"			Colonel S.D. BROWNE CB proceeded to 307 Bde HQ CROIXRAULT near POIX as President of an F.G.C.M. Capt. E. YATES attended as a member of the same Court	
"	4:4:18	6.30 am	SAA Section 61 DAC moved from BOVES to AVELESGES via CAGNY, SALEUX, CLAIRY, PISSY, SEUX, BRIQUEMESNIL, DREUIL, MONTAGNE, WARLUS, AVELESGES arriving at 4.30pm (under orders of 61 Div Q)	

2

Instructions regarding War Diaries and Intelligence Summaries are contained in F. S. Regs., Part II. and the Staff Manual respectively. Title pages will be prepared in manuscript.

WAR DIARY
or
INTELLIGENCE SUMMARY.
(*Erase heading not required.*)

Army Form C. 2118.

Place	Date	Hour	Summary of Events and Information	Remarks and references to Appendices
Refce sheet DIEPPE 16	9.4.18		The following Horses & Mules were transferred to 307 Bde { No 1 Section - 20; No 2 - 20 }	
"	10.4.18		CAPT T.R. ALSTON reported at BOVES on attachment to 58th Div Arty as assistant Staff Captain	
"	"		61 DAC (less SAA Section) moved from BEAUCAMPS le VIEUX to CROIXRAULT route LIOMER, HORNOY, THIEULLOY L'ABBAYE	
Reference sheet AMIENS 17	11.4.18		61 DAC (less SAA Section) moved from CROIXRAULT to CAGNY. Route QUEVAUVILLERS & AMIENS.	
"			2/Lieut A Robinson & 2/Lieut A.H.G. Bannister + 30 O.R. detached at D.A. Ammunition Dump as Dump Party	
"	17.4.18		2/Lieut R.A.R. Allen transferred to 307 Bde R.F.A.; 2/Lieut C.R. Bowyer transferred to 61 T.M.B's	
"	17.4.18		18 L.D. Remounts collected from Remount Depot & were distributed as follows { No 1 Section 9 L.D.; No 2 9 L.D. }	
"	20.4.18		CAPT T.R. ALSTON resumed duties of adjutant on completion of attachment to 58 Div Art as assistant Staff Captain	
"	10.4.18 – 20.4.18		2nd Lt S.J. HYDE acted as adjutant during the absence of CAPT T.R. ALSTON.	
"	20.4.18		2nd Lt S J HYDE returned to duty with No 1 Section	
"	22.4.18		The following 16 reinforcements arrived from R.A. Reinforcement Camp VERS { Gunners 18 pr 23; 4.5 2; Drivers 42 } & were divided between the Sections of the A Echelon as follows No 1 Section { 13 Gunners; 28 Drivers } No 2 Section { 12 Gunners; 14 Drivers }	
"	"		The following officers reported from 5 R.H.A. Army Bde & were posted as follows { 2nd Lt H. METCALFE No 1 Section; 2nd Lt J.H. BRIDGER No 2 Section }	
"	10.4.18	8.30 am	S.A.A. Section moved from AVELESGES to SEUX	moves under orders of 61 Div Q.
"	11.4.18		" " SEUX to ST ROCHE Station AMIENS via FERRIERES, & entrained for MERVILLE	
"	12.4.18	8.30 am	" detrained at BERGUETTE, owing to MERVILLE being in enemy hands, & proceeded to GUARBECQUE	

T2134. Wt. W708—776. 500000. 4/15. Sir J. C. & S.

3

Instructions regarding War Diaries and Intelligence Summaries are contained in F. S. Regs., Part II. and the Staff Manual respectively. Title pages will be prepared in manuscript.

WAR DIARY
or
INTELLIGENCE SUMMARY.
(Erase heading not required.)

Army Form C. 2118.

Place	Date	Hour	Summary of Events and Information	Remarks and references to Appendices
Ref. sheet AMIENS 17	24:4:18	7.45 pm	No. 1 Section DAC moved from PONT ST JEAN to ST PIERRE-a-GOUY and proceeded to HANGEST where the Section entrained with 306 Bde for BERGUETTE	
" "	25:4:18	2.30 pm	Lieut H.K. HAWSON in charge of Indian personnel marched direct from PONT ST JEAN to HANGEST where the party entrained for BERGUETTE at 6.20 am 26:4:18	
" "	"	5.30 pm	The remainder of the DAC consisting of HQ & No. 2 Section proceeded from PONT ST JEAN to ST PIERRE-a-GOUY via PONT DE METZ FERRIERES and PICQUIGNY	
" "	26:4:18	9.30 am	Headquarters D.A.C moved from ST PIERRE-a-GOUY to HANGEST & entrained with R.A.H.Q and No. 1 Coy A.S.C for BERGUETTE, the train left at 2 pm & arrived at 9.45 pm.	
" "			No. 2 Section D.A.C entrained with 307 Bde at HANGEST at intervals of 3 hrs during the day	
HAZEBROUCK 5a	26/27:4:18		on arrival at BERGUETTE HQ & Sections moved independently to following destinations — HQ Indian personnel & No. 2 Section to LIETTRES via MOLINGHEM, MAZINGHEM, ROMBLY & LINGHEM No. 1 Section to LONGHEM (S.A.A Section remained at GUARBECQUE)	
" "	29:4:18		Indian personnel distributed amongst HQ & the 3 Sections in accordance with W.E No. 818 Part VII a	
" "	"	11.30 am	Inspection of Horse lines by A.A. & Q.M.G.	
" "	"		Following postings with effect from 29.4.18 { Lieut F.G. LESITER from No. 1 to S.A.A Section; 2Lt A. ROBINSON " S.A.A Section to No. 2; 2Lt A.H.G. BANNISTER from " " No. 1	

[signature] ... Capt. Comdg 61 DAC

T2131. Wt. W708—776. 500000. 4/15. Sir J. C. & S.

Vol 25

War Diary

61st Div. Ammunition Column

May 1918.

Vol: 25.

Instructions regarding War Diaries and Intelligence Summaries are contained in F. S. Regs., Part II. and the Staff Manual respectively. Title pages will be prepared in manuscript.

WAR DIARY
or
INTELLIGENCE SUMMARY.
(Erase heading not required.)

Army Form C. 2118.

Place	Date	Hour	Summary of Events and Information	Remarks and references to Appendices
Sheet HAZEBROUCK 5a	1.5.18		Locations of HQ & Sections DAC { HQ LIETTRES; No 1 LONGHEM; No 2 LIETTRES; SAA BERGUETTE }	
"	"		The following personnel transferred from SAA Section { to 306 Bde Drivers 6 Gunners 6; 307 Bde 1 1 }	
"	"		20 Gunners attached to DTMO from Nos 1 & 2 Sections for instruction in 6 inch Newton	
"	5.5.18	8.15 pm	Headquarters moved from LIETTRES to LILLERS Route LINGHEM, ROMBLY, FONTES, NORRENT-FONTES, St HILAIRE & BOURECQ	
"	"		No 1 Section moved from LONGHEM to PONT du RÉVEILLON via ESTREE BLANCHE, AUCHY au BOIS, AMETTES	
			FERFAY, CAUCHY a la TOUR, AUCHEL LOZINGHEM ALLOUAGNE	
"	"		No 2 Section moved from LIETTRES to L'ECOUFFE Route LINGHEM, ROMBLY MAZINGHEM MOLINGHEM HAM en ARTOIS, MANQUEVILLE LILLERS	
Sheet 36a	6.5.18	2.30 pm	Headquarters moved from U 9 b 7.3 to U 17 b 3.0, HQ wagon lines to MENSECQ	
"	"		No 2 Section moved from L'ECOUFFE to ~~Bois~~ MENSECQ	
"	"		1 officer (2/Lt A A G BANNISTER) & 50 men proceeded to HAMEL DUMP (V 22 a 2.9)	
"	"		1 NCO & 2 men detailed for duty at LE TAILLY Dump V26 a and PARK DUMP U 11 d 9.2	
"	9.5.18	3 pm	HQ wagon lines moved from MENSECQ to U 9 b 7.3	
"	11.5.18		Remounts received 1 charger (Col S D Browne) 1 Rides (No 2 Section) 4 mules No 1 4 mules No 2	
"	12.5.18	6 pm	No 1 Section moved from PONT du RÉVEILLON to ALLOUAGNE (Sheet 36c C 12 b 9 6)	
"			The following officers reported for temporary duty to Bdes & were attached to Batteries as follows –	
"			{ Lieut C R LEEKE SAA Section to C/306; 2/Lt H METCALFE No 1 – B/306 } { 2/Lt A ROBINSON No 2 Section to D/307; Lt H J BRIDGER – – – C/307 }	

T2131. Wt W708–776. 500000. 4/15. Sir J. C. & S.

Instructions regarding War Diaries and Intelligence Summaries are contained in F. S. Regs., Part II. and the Staff Manual respectively. Title pages will be prepared in manuscript.

WAR DIARY
or
INTELLIGENCE SUMMARY.
(Erase heading not required.)

Army Form C. 2118.

Place	Date	Hour	Summary of Events and Information	Remarks and references to Appendices
			306 Bde: Gunners 5 No 1 Section, 5 No 2; Drivers 18 SAA; S Smiths 3 No 1; Corporals 1 No 1. 307 Bde: Gunners 7 SAA Section, 3 No 2; 10 SAA; –; 1	
Sheet 36c	13.5.18		The following personnel is posted to Brigades as follows	
	22.5.18		61 DAC relieved the 51 DAC (authority 4 D.A. operation order No 113 dated 18.5.18)	
			Moves of units as follows HQ 61 DAC from U.17 b 5.0 to O.27 a 3.8. HQ [illegible] from U.9 b 8.3 to O.20 c 9.4	
			No 1 Section from ALLOUAGNE to O.31 a Central, No 2 Section from MENSECQ to O.26 d 2.2.	
	24.5.18		2Lt BANNISTER with dump party took over the ARP at O.34 d 7.6 from 51 DAC	
	26.5.18		1 Officer (2Lt A G CLARKE No 1 Section) & 2 NCOs proceeded to Advanced Infantry R.A. Base Depot ROUEN	Correct [illegible]
	23.5.18		SAA Section moved as a result of hostile shelling in which no British personnel was killed, and [illegible] wounded & [illegible] [illegible] was moved from O.16 a 0.0 to O.15 d 2.3	
	22.5.18		On completion of relief the 61 DAC came under the orders of the [illegible] D.A. (HQ MOLINGHEM)	
	28.5.18		61 DAC [illegible] from 16 D.A. to 61 D.A. for all purposes	
	29.5.18		B.G.R.A. XI Corps inspected No 1 & 2 Sections & 61 A.R.P.	

[illegible signature]

T2134. Wt. W708—776. 500000. 4/15. Sir J. C. & S.

War Diary. Vol 26

61st Divisional Ammunition Column.

Month of June 1918.

VOL: 26.

WAR DIARY
or
INTELLIGENCE SUMMARY.
(Erase heading not required.)

Army Form C. 2118.

Instructions regarding War Diaries and Intelligence Summaries are contained in F. S. Regs., Part II. and the Staff Manual respectively. Title pages will be prepared in manuscript.

Place	Date	Hour	Summary of Events and Information	Remarks and references to Appendices
Sheet 36a			Headquarters O 27 a 3.8 (HAM-EN-ARTOIS) No 2 Section O.26.d 2.2 (HAM-EN-ARTOIS)	
			HQ Wagon lines O.20.d 2.2 " SAA Section O 15 d 2.3 (BERGUETTE)	
	1.6.18	–	No 1 Section O 31 a central (MALANOY FARM) 61 A.R.P O 34 d 8 6 (CORNET BOURDOIS)	
"	2.6.18		2Lt J H BRIDGER No 2 Section is posted to 307 Bde	Struck off strength
	3.6.18		Lt C.R. LEEKE (S A A) proceeds to England on transfer to R.A.F	
"	2.6.18		The following officers reported for 14 days attachment & are posted as follows -	
"			Lt J. C. FIELDING A/306 & 2Lt C.A. KEOGH A/306 to No 1 Section, 2Lt C F WILSON (C/307), 2Lt H T TEBBUTT (B/307)	No 2 Section
"			The following officers reported to Bdes for 14 days attachment	
			Lt J PYLE (No 1 Section) & Lt H.K. HAWSON (SAA Section) to 306 Bde 2Lt F G L COX, & 2Lt G M McCAIG to	307 Bde
"	"		2 Gunners exchanged with 306 Bde for 14 days	
"	3.6.18		5 Drivers posted to 307 Bde	
	2.6.18		2Lt A ROBINSON (No 2 Section) returned from 307 Bde on completion of 14 days attachment	
"	3.6.18		2Lt P H SKINNER [illegible] reported to S A A Section for 14 days attachment	
	10.6.18		Horse Adviser XI Corps inspected all 3 Sections horse lines	
"	12.6.18		Salvage work begun on former ammunition Dump on ROBECQ - St VENANT Road	
"	14.6.18		2Lt P H SKINNER (att SAA Section) to Reserve Army Arty School for Course in Gunnery	
"	16.6.18		The following officers returned to duty with their Bdes Lt J C FIELDING, 2Lt C F WILSON, 2Lt H T TEBBUTT	
"			Cpl A G B SPEAR (No 1 Section) awarded the Military CROSS (auth XI Corps R O No 1836 dated 8 6 18)	
"			Lieut F G LESITER (S A A Section) mentioned in despatches (auth Corps gazette)	

T2134. Wt. W708–776. 500000. 4/15. Sir J. C. & S.

Instructions regarding War Diaries and Intelligence Summaries are contained in F. S. Regs., Part II. and the Staff Manual respectively. Title pages will be prepared in manuscript.

WAR DIARY
or
INTELLIGENCE SUMMARY.
(Erase heading not required.)

Army Form C. 2118.

Place	Date	Hour	Summary of Events and Information	Remarks and references to Appendices
Sheet 36[illegible]	21.6.18		No. 846097 Serg MOWBRAY A (No. 1 Section) awarded Meritorious Service Medal (auth. Supp. to London Gazette dated 17.6.18)	(DARO 1157)
"	22.6.18		The undermentioned officers reported from the Base, and taken on strength as follows - Lieut. A/Capt. H.P SMITH (No. 1 Section), 2 Lt. J R WINTERBOTTOM (No. 2 Section)	
"	23.6.18		2 Lt. J R WINTERBOTTOM (No. 2 Section) posted to 307 Bde (vide 61 DARO No. 299)	
"	24.6.18		2 Lt. E L RANDALL posted from 16 DAC to 61 DAC with effect from ~~26~~ 23.6.18 and remains attached to XI Corps HQ. 25.6.18 - posted to S A A Section	authority G.O.C. R.A. letter SC/2/50
"	[illegible]		Lieut. A/Capt. H P SMITH (No. 1 Section) posted to 5th D.A.C (auth. R A XI Corps SC 2/52 dated 26.6.18)	
"	[illegible]		Major General F J DUNCAN CMG DSO comdg 61 Div accompanied by the G O C RA, GSO1 61 Div inspected the 3 Sections & Headquarters of the 61 D.A.C	

[illegible] Capt RFA
for Colonel, R.F.A.
Commanding 61st (S.M.) Div. Amn. Column.

61st Div. Ammn. Col. Vol 27

War Diary
– for –
July 1918.

VOL: 27.

Sheet I

Instructions regarding War Diaries and Intelligence Summaries are contained in F. S. Regs., Part II. and the Staff Manual respectively. Title pages will be prepared in manuscript.

WAR DIARY
or
INTELLIGENCE SUMMARY.
(Erase heading not required.)

Army Form C. 2118.

Place	Date	Hour	Summary of Events and Information	Remarks and references to Appendices
Sheet 36a			Headquarters O.27.a 3.8 HAM EN ARTOIS No 2 Section O.26.d 95.50 (HAM-EN-ARTOIS)	
			H.Q. Wagon lines O.20.d 2.2 " " S.A.A Section O.15.d 2.3 (BERGUETTE)	
	1.7.18		No 1 Section O.31.a Central (MALANOY FARM) · 61 A.R.P (BANNISTER DUMP) O.34.d 8.6 (CORNET BOURDOIS)	
"	"		Postings - Lieut N G ANSELL S.A.A Sect to No 1 Sect, 2/Lt J. METCALFE No 1 Sect to S.A.A Sect	
"	"		14 Drivers, 42 L.D. Horses & mules, surplus to establ. on the reduction of ammunition wagons from six to four animal teams in accordance with 1st Army letter No O.B 1866/E proceeded under the charge of an officer (2/Lt F. G. L. COX) & 2 N.C.O.s by road to BASE DEPOT BOULOGNE. Animals inspected by D.A.D.V.S at 10 am prior to departure	
"	"		Conference on the subject of Education, & the suggested formation of classes of instruction in the Division addressed by an officer from G.H.Q (attended by Colonel & Adjutant)	
"	6.7.18		CAPT T.R. ALSTON to R.A.H.Q 61 Div to act as Staff Captain during the absence on leave of MAJOR F.W.B. CRIPPS	
"	"		2/Lt S.J. HYDE No 1 Section to D.A.C H.Q to act as Adjutant during the absence of CAPT T.R. ALSTON	
"	12.7.18		61 D.A.C relieved by 74 D.A.C including personnel at BANNISTER DUMP	
"	"		61 D.A.C moved on relief to FLECHINELLE (ESTREE BLANCHE AREA) Route via St HILAIRE and LINGHEM	
"	16.7.18		COLONEL S D BROWNE C.B proceeded on a visit to BASE CAMPS at ROUEN and HAVRE	
"	7.7.18		2/Lt H.S. CLARK No 1 Section rejoined from Indian Base Depot on completion of Course	
"	11.7.18		MAJOR G HERON M.C attached to D.A.C	
"	15.7.18		2/Lt H METCALFE (S.A.A Section) attached to 61st T.M.B on probation	

Sheet 11

Instructions regarding War Diaries and Intelligence Summaries are contained in F. S. Regs., Part II. and the Staff Manual respectively. Title pages will be prepared in manuscript.

WAR DIARY
or
INTELLIGENCE SUMMARY.
(Erase heading not required.)

Army Form C. 2118.

Place	Date	Hour	Summary of Events and Information	Remarks and references to Appendices
Sheet 36a				
FLECHINELLE	13.7.18		2nd Lt G.M.McCAIG (No 2 Section) to Indian Base Depot for a Course of Instruction	
"	19.7.18		16 Surplus Drivers posted to 5th Army Reinforcement Camp at CROCQ.	
"	7.7.18		CAPT A.G.B SPEAR (No 1 Sect) assumes command of the D.A.C during the absence of COL S.D. BROWNE C.B	
"	19.7.18		COLONEL S.D. BROWNE returned from visit to BASE CAMPS, & resumed command of D.A.C vice SPEAR	
"	22.7.18		61 D.A.C moved from ESTREE BLANCHE to WARDRECQUES AREA via THEROUANNE	
WARDRECQUES AREA	"	Loc[ations]	HQ A.23. central (Fme de l'Vcmart) No 2 Section A.23 a central (BLAMART)	
Sheet 36a			No 1 Section A 23 d 8.9 do S.A.A. Section A.10 central (LE HOCQUET)	
"	23.7.18		CAPT T.R.ALSTON returned to duty as Adjutant on completion of attachment to R A H Q	
"			2nd Lt S.J. HYDE a/Adjutant returned to No 1 Section	
"	24.7.18		2nd Lt A.H.G. BANNISTER transferred from No 1 to S.A.A. Section	
"	25.7.18	3.15 pm	H.Q. D.A.C. moved from A.23 Central to A.17. a. 8. 9 (BANDRINGHEM)	
"	26.7.18	5.15 pm	61 D.A.C (less S.A.A Sect) moved from WARDRECQUES AREA to WALLON-CAPPEL - HONDEGHEM AREA	[illegible]
			Route BELLE CROIX, PONT ASQUIN EBBLINGHEM, WALLON-CAPPEL	
Sheet 27	"		Locations in new area HQ U 18. b. 1. 3 No 1 U. 18. b. 2. 6 No 2 U. 18. a. 9. 6	
"	27.7.18		306 Bde (with No 1 Sect D.A.C attached) came under the tactical orders of 1st Aust Div Arty	do
			307 No 2 9th Div Arty	

T2134. Wt. W708-776. 500000. 4/15. Sir J. C. & S.

Sheet 111

Instructions regarding War Diaries and Intelligence Summaries are contained in F. S. Regs., Part II. and the Staff Manual respectively. Title pages will be prepared in manuscript.

WAR DIARY
or
INTELLIGENCE SUMMARY.
(Erase heading not required.)

Army Form C. 2118.

Place	Date	Hour	Summary of Events and Information	Remarks and references to Appendices
Sheet 36	24.7.18		MAJOR G HERON M.C. attached for duty to 306 Bde	
"	25.7.18	2pm	M G R A 2nd ARMY inspected No 1 Section lines accompanied by G.O.C.R.A. 61 DIV	
Sheet 27	31.7.18	11pm	61 D A C moves from XV Corps back to XI Corps area (authority 61 D.A. order No 134)	(appendix A)
			H.Q. & A Echelon to FLECHINELLE via HALLON-CAPPEL, EBBLINGHEM, PONT ASQUIN, BELLE CROIX, CAUCHIE d'ECQUES, CLARQUES & THÉROUANNE	
Sheet 36a	"	9pm	S.A.A. Section as above via THEROUANNE to ESTREE-BLANCHE	

J. R. Alston Capt. (Maj)
for Colonel, R.F.A.
Commanding 61st. (S.M.) Div. Amn. Column.

T2134. Wt. W708–776. 500000. 4/15. Sir J. C. & S.

COPY No. 6

Appendix A

March Order by Colonel S.D. Browne C.B. Commanding 61st Divisional Ammn Col.

Reference map HAZEBROUCK 5a

I The 61st D.A.C. less SAA Sect. will be transferred by march route from XV to XI Corps area on night 31st July – 1st Aug.

2 The Column will move in the following order – Headquarters, No 1 Sect & No 2 Sect.

3 Starting point – present horse lines, time 11.0 pm.

4 Route to be taken will be via main HAZEBROUCK road to EBBLINGHEM – PONT ASQUIN – BELLE CROIX – CAUCHIE D'ECQUES – THÉROUANNE – ESTRÉE BLANCHE.

5 Following distances will be maintained on the line of march:–

Between Sections D.A.C. – 100 yards.
Between every 6 vehicles – 25 yards.

6 Sections will re-occupy the billets which they evacuated on July 22nd

7 The QMS. or a senior N.C.O. from each Sect. will report at D.A.C. H.Q. at 3.45. pm today to proceed by lorry to the new area.

8 Supply wagons with rations for consumption 1st prox. will accompany units, location of Refilling point on Aug. 1st will be notified later

9 All billets & horse-lines will be left clean, manure stacked on manure dump, latrines properly filled in & all cookhouse & other refuse burnt before leaving.

10 D.A.C. H.Q. will close in present area at 11.0 pm & will reopen at FLECHINELLE at the same hour.

11 ACKNOWLEDGE.

[signature]
Capt Adj

COPIES. 1 & 2 No 1 Sect
3 & 4 No 2 Sect
5 RSM
6 WAR DIARY.

CONFIDENTIAL

Vol 28

WAR DIARY

61st. D.A.C.

VOLUME 28

1st – 31st August

Instructions regarding War Diaries and Intelligence Summaries are contained in F. S. Regs., Part II. and the Staff Manual respectively. Title pages will be prepared in manuscript.

WAR DIARY
or
INTELLIGENCE SUMMARY.
(Erase heading not required.)

Army Form C. 2118.

Place	Date	Hour	Summary of Events and Information	Remarks and references to Appendices
FLECHINELLE ESTREE BLANCHE AREA	1:8:18	Wagon Croaking	61 DAC { HQ M 33 b. 15.45 No 2 M 33 b. 2.8 / No 1 M 33 b. 3.9 SAA M 33 a. 9.9	
VERCHIN	6:8:18 7:8:18		CAPT T.R. ALSTON (ADJT 61 D.A.C) attended as one of the 4 Artillery delegates for the 5 Army to revise mobilization Store Tables G 1098 (President Brig Gen E.H. WILLIS)	the Committee
FLECHINELLE Sheet 36c	7:8:18	10.30 am	61st D.A.C moved to BOESEGHEM to relieve 5 D.A.C Route BLESSY, St QUENTIN AIRE & WIDDEBROUCQ	
"	"	"	Lieut F.G. LESITER (S.A.A Section) to be acting adjutant during the absence of CAPT T.R. ALSTON on special leave to ENGLAND 8:8:18	
BOESEGHEM	"		28 Re-inforcements arrived at AIRE (4 for D.A.C remainder to Batteries)	
"	10.8.18		3 arrived for THEROUANNE, & were posted to No 2 Section D.A.C	
"	14.8.18		6 Remounts transferred to 306 Bde 3 Remounts to 307 Bde	
	9.8.18		Lt W.P. BOULTON (5 Aus Arty) posted to No 2 Section 61 D.A.C, to remain attached to XI Corps HQ	
	13.8.18		15 Re-inforcements arrived at AIRE, & were posted as follows { 306 - 1 Sergt: 1 Corpl / 307 - 1 : 10 Gunners / D.A.C - 1 Bdr : 1 Driver	
"	12:8:18		The undermentioned N.C.O's, were despatched to HAVRE for ENGLAND on 6 months Home Duty R.S.M THORNTON (Headquarters) B.S.M. PARKER (SAA) Sgt MARGISON (S.A.A)	
	11:8:18		Lieut H SUTHERLAND reported for duty & was posted to S.A.A Section	

T2134. Wt. W708—776. 500000. 4/15. Sir J. C. & S.

Instructions regarding War Diaries and Intelligence Summaries are contained in F. S. Regs., Part II. and the Staff Manual respectively. Title pages will be prepared in manuscript.

WAR DIARY
or
INTELLIGENCE SUMMARY.
(Erase heading not required.)

Army Form C. 2118.

Place	Date	Hour	Summary of Events and Information	Remarks and references to Appendices
Sheet 36a			Postings: Lt H. BUCKETT from S A A Section to No 1 Section	
BOESEGHEM	15.8.18		2Lt S. J. HYDE " No 1 " S.A.A. "	
"	14.8.18		2Lt H METCALFE (S.A.A. Section) to 61st T M Batteries (auth. [illegible] R © 1209)	
"	19.8.18	1.20 pm	No 1 Section & CC moves from BOESEGHEM to CORNET-BRASSART (O 23 C 5.2) & come under the orders of G.O.C R.A 74 Div for purposes of ammunition supply	
"	21.8.18		Lt T S WOOD & 12 Re inforcements arrives at AIRE & were posted as follows – 306 Bde – 3 Gunners, 4 Drivers 307 Bde – Lt T. S. WOOD & 2 Gunners D.A.C. – 3 Drivers	
"	22.8.18	11 am	General ELLIOTT (military adviser to the Indian Army) inspected all Indian personnel in S A A Section lines	
"	23.8.18		Lt E W. TUNBRIDGE (61st T M B's) posted to No 1 Section D A C, while doing duty as Temp [illegible] officer to the 61st Div Arty	
"	22.8.18		S.A.A Section moves from BOESEGHEM to TANNAY (I. 30.c 7.3)	
"	23.8.18		Lt F. G LESITER acting adjutant returns to S.A.A Section for duty on the return from leave of CAPT T R. ALSTON	
"	26.8.18		No 1 Section moves from O.23.c 5.2 to I.7 c 3.2 & ceases to be under the orders of 74 D.A for any purposes	
"	27.8.18	10 am	The following ammunition refilling points taken over from 59 D.A C (1) 59 A.R.P. – STEENBECQUE C 30 c 8.8 (2) advanced ARP – CAUDESCURE K 7 d 1.0	
"	28.8.18		No 2 Section moves from BOESEGHEM to TANNAY I 29 d 6.4	
"	29.8.18		Lt P. BEW 74 Div Arty is posted to No 1 Section D.A.C, & to remain attached to H.Q. XI Corps.	
"	30.8.18		Construction of new A.R.P. at K 7 d 8.8. begun	

T. R. Alston Capt for Colonel, R.F.A.
Commanding C.st. (S.M.) Div. Amn. Column

T2134. Wt. W708–776. 500000. 4/15. Sir J. C. & S.

61st Divisional Ammunition Column.

Vol 29

War Diary

— for —

September 1918.

VOL: 29.

Instructions regarding War Diaries and Intelligence Summaries are contained in F. S. Regs., Part II. and the Staff Manual respectively. Title pages will be prepared in manuscript.

WAR DIARY
or
INTELLIGENCE SUMMARY.
(Erase heading not required.)

Army Form C. 2118.

Place	Date	Hour.	Summary of Events and Information	Remarks and references to Appendices
Sheet 36a		Map locations	HQ I.8.c.6.0, No 1 I.7.c.3.3. BOESEGHEM; No 2 I.29.d.6.4 TANNAY; S.A.A. I.30.c.7.3 (TANNAY); A.R.P. (STEENBECQUE) C.30.c.8.8; A.R.P. (le FORET) J.25.a.5.0.; D.B.S. I.29.a.1.7. Dump A.R.P. K.7.d.9.0 (CAUDESCURE); Nos 61 A.R.P. K.7.d.8.8 (under construction)	
BOESEGHEM	1.9.18		Lieut E. P. MICKLEWOOD 59 D.A.C. reported for duty & was posted to No 2 Section	
"	3.9.18		The following moves carried out, HQ to J.21.a.2.6, HQ wagon lines to J.21.d.95.40, No 1 Section to J.33.b.7.5	
Sheet 36a	4.9.18		A.R.P. formed at NEUF BERQUIN L.14.c.3.8. (Officer i/c 2/Lt F.G.L. COX)	
"	"	10 am	61 D.A.C. moved to ARREWAGE AREA all via CROIX MARRAISSE & VIA ROMA	
			new locations HQ K.8.c.4.3, No 1 Section ITCHIN Fm K.10.d.6.6, No 2 Section BONAR Fm K.16.a.7.9, S.A.A. Section TAXI Fm K.9.d.1.4	
"	"	2.15 pm	No 2 Section D.A.C. moved from BONAR Fm to L.7.c.7.8	
"	5.9.18	7.15 pm	S.A.A. Section D.A.C. moved from TAXI Fm to NEUF BERQUIN L.14.c.8.9	
"	7.9.18		No 1 Section D.A.C. moved from ITCHIN Fm to K.10.a.8.1	
"	8.9.18	10.30 am	HQ D.A.C. moved from K.8.c.4.3 to L.20.c.7.0 Route via MERVILLE	
"	10.9.18		Lieut E. P. MICKLEWOOD (No 2 Section) & 4 O.R. to 2nd Army T.M. School	
"	11.9.18		Section of 6 18 pr wagons (No 1 Section) attached to No 2 Section for ammunition supply to B/306 (location L.7.c.7.8)	
"	14.9.18		No 1 Section (less 6 18 pr 2.4.5. & 1 G.S. wagon detailed for salvage work) moved to NEUF BERQUIN AREA L.21.d.8.8.	
"	18.9.18		2 Lt S. J. HYDE attached to 307 Bde for duty	
"	21.9.18		2 Lt H. S. CLARKE relieved 2 Lt F.G.L. COX as officer i/c RING DUMP (NEUF BERQUIN)	
"	23.9.18		Lt H. G. ANSELL & party at ANSELL DUMP relieved by XI Corps	

T2131. Wt. W708—776. 500000. 4/15. Sir J. C. & S.

Instructions regarding War Diaries and Intelligence Summaries are contained in F. S. Regs., Part II. and the Staff Manual respectively. Title pages will be prepared in manuscript.

WAR DIARY
or
INTELLIGENCE SUMMARY.
(Erase heading not required.)

Army Form C. 2118.

Place	Date	Hour	Summary of Events and Information	Remarks and references to Appendices
Sheet 36 "	27.9.18		Lt F. G. LESITER appointed to command (temp'y) of S.A.A. Section vice Capt R.G.B. CHASE to INDIAN BASE DEPT ROUEN	
"	28.9.18		CAPT T. R. ALSTON " " " " 61 D.A.C. " COLONEL S.D. BROWNE - ENGLAND (on leave)	
"	"		Lt A. J. PYLE " " " " No 1 Section " CAPT A.G.B. SPEAR " "	

T. R. Alston Capt.
R.F.A.
Commanding 61st (S.M.) Div. Amn. Column

T2134. Wt. W708–776. 500000. 4/15. Sir J. C. & S.

78

Vol 30

61st Divisional Ammunition Column.

War Diary

— for —

October 1918.

VOL: 30.

Army Form C. 2118.

Instructions regarding War Diaries and Intelligence Summaries are contained in F. S. Regs., Part II. and the Staff Manual respectively. Title pages will be prepared in manuscript.

WAR DIARY
or
INTELLIGENCE SUMMARY.
(Erase heading not required.)

Place	Date	Hour	Summary of Events and Information	Remarks and references to Appendices
Sheet 36ᴺ	1:10.18	map location	HQ L.20.c.7.0 / No 1 L.21.d.8.8 / No 2 L.7.c.7.8 / SAA L.14.c.6.9 / ARP (RING DUMP) L.14.c.3.8	
"	"		CAPT T.R. ALSTON to RAHQ as Staff Captain during the absence on leave of MAJOR F.W.N. CRIPPS	
"	"		CAPT E. YATES (No 2 Section) appointed to temp. command of D.A.C vice CAPT T.R. ALSTON	
"	"		2/Lt S.J. HYDE (SAA Section) appointed acting adjutant D.A.C vice CAPT T.R. ALSTON	
"	"		Lt G.H. GIBBS appointed to command of No 2 Section D.A.C vice Capt E. YATES	
"	4.10.18	10 am	61 DAC on relief by 59 DAC moves to MAZINGHEM Route MERVILLE CALONNE ST VENANT GUARBECQUE	appendix A
	6-7 .10.18		61 DAC entrains at BERGUETTE THIENNES & STEENBECQUE for DOULLENS & ROSEL Fme	
Refce sheet LENS 11	7.10.18		on detrainment 61 D.A.C proceeds to AMPLIER	
"	8.10.18	7 am	61 DAC left AMPLIER for RIVIERE GROSVILLE Route HALLOY, POMMERA, MONDICOURT, La BELLEVUE BEAUMETZ	appendix B
"	9.10.18	8.30 am	61 DAC left RIVIERE GROSVILLE for ST LEGER Route BRETENCOURT, BLAIREVILLE, FICHEUX, BOISLEUX au MONT HAMELINCOURT to MOULIN de ST LEGER (time of arrival 12 noon)	appendix C
	10.10.18	7.30 a	61 DAC left ST LEGER for LAGNICOURT Route CROISILLES, ECOUST ST MEIN, NOREUIL LAGNICOURT	appendix D
Sheet 57C	"		map location D.A.C H.Q C.30.b.6.9	
"	11.10.18	8.30 am	61 DAC moves from C.30.b & d to E.28.a & b on N. side of BAPAUME-CAMBRAI Rd [map location of D.A.C HQ E.28.b.5.8]	appendix E
"	1.10.18		2/Lt S.J. HYDE (S.A.A. Section) returned on completion of tour of duty with B/306 Bty	
"	2.10.18		2/Lt G.M. McCAIG (No 2 Section) reported to B/306 Bty for duty vice HYDE	
"	10.10.18		CAPT T.R. ALSTON resumes command of 61 DAC on return of MAJOR F.W.N. CRIPPS S.C.R.A. 61 Dn vice YATES who proceeded on leave to U.K.	

T2134. Wt. W708–776. 500000. 4/15. Sir J. C. & S.

Instructions regarding War Diaries and Intelligence Summaries are contained in F. S. Regs., Part II. and the Staff Manual respectively. Title pages will be prepared in manuscript.

WAR DIARY
or
INTELLIGENCE SUMMARY.
(Erase heading not required.)

Army Form C. 2118.

Place	Date	Hour	Summary of Events and Information	Remarks and references to Appendices
Sheet 57c	10.10.18		CAPT T.R. ALSTON resumes the duties of ADJT vice HYDE, who returns to S.A.A. Section for duty	
"	"		Dump of SAA & grenades at ANNEUX taken over by O/C SAA Section	
VALENCIENNES 12	13.10.18		61 DAC (less SAA Section, which remained at E.28.a sheet 57c) moved to Fbg ST ROCH N.E. of CAMBRAI, Route FONTAINE NOTRE DAME, CANTIMPRE (map locations HQ. A.6.d.0.2 No 1 A.6.c.9.1. No 2 A.6.d.2.4 Sheet 57b)	Appendix F
Sheet 57b	"		Lt E.P. MICKEWOOD (No 2 Section) reported for duty to 306 Bde, 2Lt S.J. HYDE (SAA) posted for temp. duty to No 2 Section	
"	"		2Lt H.S. CLARKE (No 1 Sect) & party of 15 O.R. took over A.R.P. from 40th D.A.C at B.6.c.5.2	
Sheet 57b 51a	15.10.18		61 DAC (less SAA Section) moved from A.6.c & d to valley S. of RIEUX Route CAMBRAI-NAVES – CAMBRAI-SOLESMES Roads	Appendix G
"	"		Locations HQ U.26.a.2.1 No 1 U.25.d.9.8 No 2 U.25.b.9.4	
"	"		2Lt H.S. CLARKE & party opened new A.R.P. at U.23.a.4.1	
"	17.10.18		A.R.P. at U.23.a.4.1 closed, and Dump at C.3.b & 6 re-opened	
"	18.10.18		2Lt G.M. McCAIG died of wounds received in action with C/306 Bty & was buried 19.10.18 at Cemetery A.12.b	Sheet 57b
"	19.10.18		2Lt H.S. CLARKE & party (less 8 men) relieved at C.3.b Dump by 19th D.A.	
"	14.10.18		Colonel S.D. BROWNE on return from leave, resumes Command of 61 DAC vice ALSTON	
Sheet 57c	16.10.18		SAA Section 61 DAC moved from E.28.a to CANTAING (L.3.a.9.2) via GRAINCOURT	
Sheet 57c & 57b	19.10.18		" " " " L.3.a.9.3 to C.3.a.7.6 via PROVILLE CAMBRAI & CAUROIR	
Sheet 51a	21.10.18		61 DAC (less SAA Section) moved to U.29 via CAMBRAI-SOLESMES Road. Map locations: HQ U.29.d.5.3; No 1 U.29.d.6.4; No 2 U.29.b central (ST AUBERT STATION)	

T2134. Wt. W708—776. 500000. 4/15. Sir J. C. & S.

Instructions regarding War Diaries and Intelligence Summaries are contained in F. S. Regs., Part II. and the Staff Manual respectively. Title pages will be prepared in manuscript.

WAR DIARY
or
INTELLIGENCE SUMMARY.
(Erase heading not required.)

Army Form C. 2118.

Place	Date	Hour	Summary of Events and Information	Remarks and references to Appendices
Sheet 51a	23.10.18	2.30 p	61 DAC HQ moves from U 29 d 5 3 to U 24 a 5.7 (ST AUBERT)	
"	"		SAA Section 61 DAC moves from C.3.a.7.6 to V.19.a.6.9 (ST AUBERT)	
"	25.10.18		" " " " " V.19 a 6.9 (ST AUBERT) to P 33.b.6.9 MONTRÉCOURT	
"	26.10.18		HQ & A Echelon 61 DAC moved from ST AUBERT to MONTRÉCOURT. Map Locations: HQ P 33. d. 3. 2; No 1 P 33. d. 75.20; No 2 V. 4. a 80.15	Appendix H
"	16.10.18		Lieut E.P. MICKLEWOOD (No 2 Section) attached 306 Bde wounded in action & struck off strength	
"	27.10.18		Lieut/CAPT. E. YATES (No 2 Section) returned from leave & resumed command of No 2 Section vice GIBBS	

for [signature] Capt. Adj.

T2134. Wt. W708–776. 500000. 4/15. Sir J. C. & S.

Vol 31

61st Divisional Ammunition Column.

War Diary

— for —

November 1918.

VOL: 31.

Instructions regarding War Diaries and Intelligence Summaries are contained in F. S. Regs., Part II. and the Staff Manual respectively. Title pages will be prepared in manuscript.

WAR DIARY
or
INTELLIGENCE SUMMARY.
(Erase heading not required.)

Army Form C. 2118.

Place	Date	Hour	Summary of Events and Information	Remarks and references to Appendices
Sheet 51[a]	1.11.18	Map Location	Headquarters P.33.d.3.2 No 2 Section V.4.a.20.15 No 1 Section P.33.d.75.20 S.A.A Section P.33.b.6.9	
" "	3.11.18		S.A.A Section 61 D.A.C moves from SAULZOIR to ST AUBERT (V.19.a.5.8)	
" "	4.11.18		HQ & A Echelon 61 D.A.C moves from MONTRÉCOURT to BERMERAIN. Map Locations: HQ Q.22.c.9.3; No 1 Q.22.c.8.4; No 2 Q.22.d.05.25	Appendix A
" "	"		S.A.A Section 61 D.A.C moves from ST AUBERT to HAUSSY (V.18.a.2.8)	
" "	5.11.18	12.30 pm	HQ & A Echelon 61 D.A.C moves from BERMERAIN to MARESCHES via SEPMERIES (Map location L.25.d.6.6)	Appendix B
" "	"		Personnel at A.R.P (Q.13.a) consisting of 1 NCO, 8 OR 61 D.A.C moves to ARP at L.21.c	Appendix C
Sheet 51	7.11.18	2 pm	HQ & No 1 Section 61 D.A.C moves from MARESCHES to WARGNIES le Petit Route VILLERS POL, MAISON BLANCHE	
" "	"		Map location of S.A.C HQ G.28.c.6.2 A.R.P opened at G.22.d	
" "	8.11.18		HQ 61 D.A.C moves to WARGNIES X Rds G.22.c.95.20	
" "	2.11.18		Lieut F.G. LESITER (acting O/C S.A.A Section) proceeds on leave to ENGLAND Lt H.K HANSON assumes Command	
" "	7.11.18		Lt (A/Capt) R.G.B CHASE returned from Course at INDIAN BASE DEPOT & resumes Command of S.A.A Section	
" "	9.11.18	10.00	No 2 Section 61 D.A.C moves from MARESCHES to WARGNIES le Petit (Map location G.22.c.4.2)	
" "		14.30	No 1 " " " WARGNIES le Petit to BAVAY AREA (Map Location I.26.a.3.6)	
" "	10.11.18	10.00	HQ 61 D.A.C moves from WARGNIES le Petit to LOUVIGNIES-BAVAY I.26.c.3.3 via ST WAAST-la-VALLÉE	
" "	"	14.00	No 2 Section 61 D.A.C moves from WARGNIES le Petit to BAVAY - TAISNIERES Rd (I.20.b.9.6)	
51[a]			S.A.A Section 61 D.A.C moves from HAUSSY to VENDEGIES (Q.14.b.3.8)	

F. Lesiter
Lieut Adjt
61st DAC for General Command[illegible]

T2131. Wt. W708-776. 500000. 4/15. Sir J. C. & S.

Instructions regarding War Diaries and Intelligence Summaries are contained in F. S. Regs., Part II. and the Staff Manual respectively. Title pages will be prepared in manuscript.

WAR DIARY
or
INTELLIGENCE SUMMARY.
(Erase heading not required.)

Army Form C. 2118.

Place	Date	Hour	Summary of Events and Information	Remarks and references to Appendices
Sheet No				
	16.11.18		CAPTAIN R.G.B. CHASE (O.C. SAA Section) proceeded on leave to ENGLAND – Lt H.K. HAWSON assumed command	[initials]
Sheet 51 & 51A	16.11.18	0930 hrs	H.Q. DAC & "A" echelon moved from "BAVAY AREA" to WARGNIES-LE-PETIT – route through main street of BAVAY	[initials]
"	17.11.18	1015 hrs	H.Q. DAC & "A" echelon moved from WARGNIES-LE-PETIT AREA to VENDIGIES – route – VILLERS POL – CHAUSSE – BRUNEHAUT – CARBLIN – VENDIGIES.	[initials]
"	18.11.18	1030 hrs	H.Q. DAC & "A" echelon moved from VENDIGIES to St VAAST – route – St MARTIN – MAISON BLEUE – HAUSSY – St VAAST.	[initials]
1/100,000 VALENCIENNES	19.11.18	1030 hrs	H.Q. DAC & "A" echelon moved from St VAAST to CAMBRAI (main Town) – route – road junction E.4. 85.32 & thence by main road entering the town at Bridge under railway at C.4. 85.15.	[initials]
LENS II 1/100,000 VALENCIENNES 1/100,000	23.11.18	1015 hrs	H.Q. DAC & "A" echelon moved from CAMBRAI (main Town) to an area near DOULLENS (BEUGNATRE) – route – via FREMICOURT	[initials]
1/100,000 LENS II	24.11.18	1015 hrs	D.A.C with "A" & "B" echelons moved from BEUGNATRE to BIENVILLERS – route SAPIGNES – BIRUCOURT – ACHIET-LE-GRAND – BUCQUOY – ESSARTS – HANNESCAMP.	[initials]
"	25.11.18	0730 hrs	D.A.C with "A" & "B" echelons moved from BIENVILLERS to NEUILLY-LE-DIEN – ACQUET – LANNOY – route POMMIER – HAMBERCAMP – GAUDIEMORE – DOULLENS thence by main road to AUXI-LE-CHATEAU	[initials] [initials]
			Location of units. D.A.C.H.Q. and SAA Section at ACQUET – No 1 Section at LANNOY. No 2 Section at NEUILLY-LE-DIEN	
"	27.11.18	–	No 2 Section DAC moved from NEUILLY-LE-DIEN to WILLENCOURT.	[initials]
"	28.11.18	1045 hrs	H.Q. DAC moved from ACQUET to LA-NEUVILLE	[initials]
"	"	1030 hrs	No 1 Section DAC moved from LANNOY to VILLEROY-SUR-AUTHIE.	[initials]

[signature] Lieut. & Adjt. for Lt. Colonel Comdg 1st Canadian DAC

T2134. Wt. W708–776. 500000. 4/15. Sir J. C. & S.

61st Divisional Ammunition Column.

VR 32

War Diary

— for —

December 1918.

Vol: 32.

Instructions regarding War Diaries and Intelligence Summaries are contained in F. S. Regs., Part II. and the Staff Manual respectively. Title pages will be prepared in manuscript.

WAR DIARY
or
INTELLIGENCE SUMMARY.
(Erase heading not required.)

Army Form C. 2118.

Place	Date	Hour	Summary of Events and Information	Remarks and references to Appendices
SHEET LENS 1/100,000	8.12.18	1430hrs	The G.O.C 61st Division visited 61st D.A.C at LANEUVILLE & inspected the animals, & Billets of the men of No1 Section at VILLEROY-SUR-AUTHIE. No2 Section at WILLENCOURT & No3 Section at ACQUET.	
	11.12.18	1400hrs	The G.O.C.R.A. IIIrd Army visited 61st D.A.C at LANEUVILLE & inspected the animals & Billets of the men of No1 Section at VILLEROY-SUR-AUTHIE. No2 Section at WILLENCOURT & No3 Section at ACQUET	
	15.12.18	1500hrs	No3 (S.A.A.) Section moved from ACQUET to LE PONCHEL.	
	17.12.18	"	LIEUT. H. BUCKETT (No3 (SAA) Section) posted to R.H.&R.F.A Base Depot LE HAVRE	
	"		CAPTAIN. E. O. YATES granted leave to U.K via BOULOGNE. LIEUT. G.H. GIBBS assumed command of No2 Section	
	21.12.18	—	LIEUT. F. G. LESITER appointed Adjutant with rank of A/CAPTAIN from 28.11.18 vice A/CAPTAIN. T. R. ALSTON evacuated sick to ENGLAND.	
	"		LIEUT. R. A. N. SHUTTE attached to 61st D.A.C & temporarily attached to No2 Section	
	25.12.18		LIEUT. H. K. HAWSON (No3 (SAA) Section) granted leave to ENGLAND	
	28.12.18		LIEUT. G. H. GIBBS (acting O.C No2 Section) granted leave to ENGLAND. 2nd LIEUT. F. G. L. COX assumed command of No2 Section.	
	"		LIEUT. R. A. N. SHUTTE posted to 310 Army Field Artillery Brigade.	

F. Lesiter Capt & Adjt
for Colonel, R.F.A.
Commanding 61st. (S.M.) Div. Amn. Column

61st Div. Ammunition Column.   Vol 33

War Diary

— for —

January 1919.

—

Vol: 33.

Instructions regarding War Diaries and Intelligence Summaries are contained in F. S. Regs., Part II. and the Staff Manual respectively. Title pages will be prepared in manuscript.

WAR DIARY
or
INTELLIGENCE SUMMARY.
(Erase heading not required.)

Army Form C. 2118.

Place	Date	Hour	Summary of Events and Information	Remarks and references to Appendices
SHEET LENS 1/100,000	3.1.19	-	CAPTAIN. E.O. YATES returned from leave & resumed Command of No 2 Section 61. D.A.C.	(initialled)
	13.1.19	0930hrs	51 x "Y" Horses despatched to No 3 Base Remount Depôt DIEPPE (Authority R.A.G. 517/14)	(initialled)
	20.1.19	0930hrs	10 x "Y" Horses despatched to No 3 Base Remount Depôt DIEPPE (A " " ")	(initialled)
	26.1.19		COLONEL. S.D. BROWNE. C.B. R.A left the 61 D.A.C to take over Command of III Army Animal Collecting Camp at CANDAS.	(initialled)
	"		2nd LIEUT. F.G.L. COX left the 61 D.A.C to proceed to III Army Animal Collecting Camp to act as Camp Adjutant.	(initialled)
	"		CAPTAIN. E.O. YATES assumed temporary Command of 61st D.A.C vice COLONEL. S.D. BROWNE C.B.R.A. to III Army Animal Collecting Camp.	(initialled)
	28.1.19		LIEUT. G.H. GIBBS returned from leave took over Command of No 2 Section 61 D.A.C vice CAPTAIN. E.O. YATES to command 61. D.A.C.	(initialled)

F. Tesiter
Captain & Adjutant,
61st (S.M.) Divisional Amn. Column.

for Captain.
Commanding 61st. (S.M.) Div. Amn. Column.

T2134. Wt. W708—776. 500000. 4/15. Sir J. C. & S.

19

Instructions regarding War Diaries and Intelligence Summaries are contained in F. S. Regs., Part II. and the Staff Manual respectively. Title pages will be prepared in manuscript.

WAR DIARY
or
INTELLIGENCE SUMMARY.
(Erase heading not required.)

Army Form C. 2118.

Vol 34

Place	Date	Hour	Summary of Events and Information	Remarks and references to Appendices
SHEET LENS 1,100.000	1·2·19	1030 hrs	80 x Animals transferred to 307 Brigade R.F.A.	(initialled)
	7·2·19	"	LIEUT. A.J. PYLE proceeded with Dispersal Draft to CANDAS for Demobilization	(initialled)
	8·2·19		LIEUT. E.L. RAGGETT proceeded with Dispersal Draft to CANDAS for Demobilization	(initialled)
	8·2·19		LIEUT. B.S. GORTON (late T.M. BATTERIES) posted to 61. D.A.C (authority RAQ 200/117 d/d 11.2.19)	(initialled)
	10·2·19		CAPTAIN. A.J. GARLAND proceeded with Dispersal Draft to CANDAS for Demobilization	(initialled)
	20·2·19		6 x "Z" Horses despatched to No 5 Veterinary Hospital ABBEVILLE	(initialled)
	21·2·19		2nd LIEUT. A.G. BANNISTER proceeded with Dispersal Draft to CANDAS for Demobilization	(initialled)
	21·2·19		1 x "Z" Horse & 5 x "Z" mules were sold by auction in AUXI-LE-CHATEAU	(initialled)
	28·2·19		4 x "Z" mules & 2 x "Z" Horses despatched to AUXI-LE-CHATEAU for sale by auction.	(initialled)

[illegible] Capt. & Adjt.
for Major,
R.F.A.
Commanding 61st (S.M.) Div. Am. Column.

Instructions regarding War Diaries and Intelligence Summaries are contained in F. S. Regs., Part II. and the Staff Manual respectively. Title pages will be prepared in manuscript.

WAR DIARY
or
INTELLIGENCE SUMMARY.
(Erase heading not required.)

Army Form C. 2118. 61

Vol 35

Place	Date	Hour	Summary of Events and Information	Remarks and references to Appendices
LENS SHEET 1.100.000	1.3.19	0900hrs	4 x "Z" L.D. Horses & 2 x "Z" L.D. Mules sent to 31 Mobile Veterinary Section BERNAVILLE	
	3.3.19	0900 "	34 x "Z" L.D. Mules sent to No5 Advanced Remount Squadron ABBEVILLE	
	4.3.19	0900 "	80 x "X" L.D. Mules sent to Corps Animal Collecting Camp BEAUVAL.	
	5.3.19	0915 "	5 x "Y" Ride Horses sent to Corps Animal Collecting Camp BEAUVAL.	
	7.3.19	0930 "	5 x "Z" L.D. Mules sent to No2 Advanced Remount Depôt ABBEVILLE	
	"	0900 "	10 x "X" L.D. Horses sent to No14 Veterinary Hospital ABBEVILLE.	
	"	0930	2 x "Z" Ride Horses & 5 x "Z" L.D. Mules sent to No1 Coy R.A.S.C for sale by auction at AUXI-LE-CHATEAU	
	10.3.19	0900 "	25 x "X" L.D. Mules & 9 x "X" Ride Horses despatched to IIIrd Army Animal Camp CANDAS.	
	12.3.19	0915 "	3 x "X" L.D. Horses sent to No14 V.E.S. ABBEVILLE.	
	13.3.19	—	CAPTAIN. A.G.B. SPEAR. M.C (O.C. No1 Section) proceeded on leave to U.K. for 14 days.	
	"	—	LIEUTENANT. H.G. ANSELL assumed command of No1 Section during absence of CAPT: SPEAR.	
	14.3.19	1400hrs	CAPTAIN. T.S. STAFFORD (R.A.M.C.) proceeded independantly to ENGLAND for final demobilization	
	"		" A.W. ADAMS (RAMC) 61st Division took over duties of MO. to 61. DAC vice CAPT. STAFFORD.	
	"	0915 "	7 x "C" Rides despatched to Corps Animal Collecting Camp. BEAUVAL	
	17.3.19	"	6 x "X" Ride despatched to IIIrd Army Animal Collecting Camp. CANDAS.	
	22.3.19	"	53 x "X" Mules despatched to Corps. A.C. Camp BEAUVAL.	

Ceased

Army Form C. 2118.

Instructions regarding War Diaries and Intelligence Summaries are contained in F. S. Regs., Part II. and the Staff Manual respectively. Title pages will be prepared in manuscript.

WAR DIARY
or
INTELLIGENCE SUMMARY.
(Erase heading not required.)

Place	Date	Hour	Summary of Events and Information	Remarks and references to Appendices
LENS SHEET 1.100,000	24.3.19	1000hrs	61. D.A.C moved from area WEST of AUXI-LE-CHATEAU to OUTREBOIS	
			61 D.A.C. H.Q. from LA NEUVILLE to OUTREBOIS	
			No 2 Section " WILLENCOURT to "	
			No 1 " " VILLEROY SUR AUTHIE to "	
			No 3 (SAA) " " LE PONCHEL to "	
	24.3.19		2/LIEUT. A. J. ROBINSON transferred from 306 Brigade R.F.A. to 61. D.A.C (Authority R.A.G. 200/17)	
	26.3.19	0915 hrs	5 x "X" Ride Horses & 13 x "X" L.D. Horses sent to Third Army A. C. Camp CANDAS.	
	28.3.19	-	LIEUT: H. S. CLARKE struck off strength of 61 D.A.C & taken on strength of General Indian Base Depot MARSEILLES from 24.3.19 (Authority AG 2333/2(O)/1 24.3.19)	
	"		LIEUT. B. S. GORTON proceeded to U.K. for final Demobilization	

[signature] Capt & Adjt
for Major R.F.A.
Commanding 61st. (S.M.) Div. Amn. Column.

T2134. Wt. W708-776. 500000. 4/15. Sir J. C. & S.

61 D Am Col 61

Army Form C. 2118.

Instructions regarding War Diaries and Intelligence Summaries are contained in F. S. Regs., Part II. and the Staff Manual respectively. Title pages will be prepared in manuscript.

WAR DIARY
or
INTELLIGENCE SUMMARY.
(Erase heading not required.)

April 36

Place	Date	Hour	Summary of Events and Information	Remarks and references to Appendices
LENS SHEET 1/100,000	5.4.19		CAPTAIN F. G. LESITER attached to 19th D.A.C	F.G.L.
	"		CAPTAIN R. G. B. CHASE attached to 19th D.A.C	F.G.L.
	"		LIEUT. S. J. HYDE attached to 19th D.A.C	F.G.L.
	"		CAPTAIN C. A. STATHAM (19th D.A.C) attached to 61st D.A.C, posted on 26.4.19	Authority XVII Corps O.P. A 48/951
	"		LIEUT. W. E. KINGWELL (19th D.A.C) attached to 61st D.A.C., posted on 26.4.19	— Do —
	"		2/LIEUT F. W. SUTTON attached to 61. D.A.C. & granted leave to U.K. 22.4.19	F.G.L.
	9.4.19		LIEUT. A. G. ANSELL posted to Army of Occupation	F.G.L.
	20.4.19		143 Indian Personnel despatched to NEUVE-CHATEL to form a "Z" Horse Depot for Demobilization.	F.G.L.
	25.4.19		CAPTAIN. A. G. B. SPEAR M.C. proceeded to U.K for final Demobilization &	F.G.L.
			LIEUT. A. BAKER took over command of No 1 Section vice CAPT. SPEAR.	F.G.L.
	21.4.19		LIEUT. A. BAKER (307 Brigade) transferred to 61. D.A.C.	F.G.L.
	24.4.19		CAPTAIN. F. G. LESITER returns from 14 days leave to the U.K. & resumes his duties as Adjutant 61. D.A.C.	F.G.L.
	30.4.19		76 x "X" mules despatched to ~~Third~~ Army Animal Camp CANDAS.	F.G.L.

F. Lesiter Capt & Adjt
for Major R.F.A.
Commanding 61st. (S.M.) Div. Amn. Column

Army Form C. 2118.

Instructions regarding War Diaries and Intelligence Summaries are contained in F. S. Regs., Part II. and the Staff Manual respectively. Title pages will be prepared in manuscript.

WAR DIARY
or
INTELLIGENCE SUMMARY.
(Erase heading not required.)

61 D Am Col

37

Place	Date	Hour	Summary of Events and Information	Remarks and references to Appendices
LENS 1.100,000 SHEET	6.5.19		MAJOR. E. YATES granted 14 days leave to U.K.	FR
	"		CAPTAIN. F.G. LESITER takes over command 61 D.A.C during absence of MAJOR. YATES on leave	FR
	10.5.19		15 O.R. despatched to U.K for final demobilization	FR
	14.5.19		14 O.R. despatched to U.K. for final demobilization	FR
	13.5.19		LIEUT. W.E KINGWELL granted 14 days leave to U.K.	FR
	14.5.19		2/LIEUT. F.W. SUTTON returns from leave & takes over temporary command of No 3 Section vice LIEUT. KINGWELL on leave	FR
	17.5.19		8 O.R's. despatched to U.K for final demobilization	FR
	20.5.19		LIEUT. A. BAKER granted 14 days leave to U.K.	FR
	22.5.19		2/LIEUT. F.W. SUTTON proceeded to "Z" Horse Depot ~~NEUFCHATEL~~. ROUEN	FR
	"		CAPT: F.G.L. COX proceeded from IIIrd Army Animal Camp CANDAS to "Z" Horse Depot NEUFCHATEL.	FR
	24.5.19		MAJOR. E. YATES returned from leave & resumed command of 61. D.A.C.	FR
	26.5.19		CAPT: G.H. GIBBS granted 14 days leave to U.K.	FR
	29.5.19		LIEUT. W.E. KINGWELL returns from leave & resumes command of No 3 (S.A.A.) Section.	FR
	31.5.19		MAJOR. E. RIMMER inspected the Animal Account for May of the 61 D.A.C.	FR

F. Lester Capt & Adjt
for Major R.F.A.
Commanding 61st. (S.M.) Div. Amn. Column

F2134. Wt. W708–776. 500000. 4/15. Sir J. C. & S.

www.ingramcontent.com/pod-product-compliance
Lightning Source LLC
Chambersburg PA
CBHW081405160426
43193CB00013B/2114